Dr. JAC's™

Guide to Writing with Depth

Dr.JAC's<sup>TM</sup>

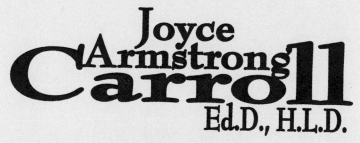

*Guide to Writing with Depth*

# Joyce Armstrong Carroll
### Ed.D., H.L.D.

Absey & Co.
Spring, Texas

"Friendship is almost always the union of a part of one mind with a part of another: People are friends in spots."

--George Santayana

I dedicate this book to my friend Megan Chill; she has been my friend in just the right spots.

Requests for permission to make copies of any part of the work should be mailed to
Permissions
Absey & Co. Inc.
23011 Northcrest
Spring, TX 77389
888-412-2739

Library of Congress Control Number: 2002092456

Carroll, Joyce Armstrong, 1937-
    Dr. JAC's Guide to Writing with Depth/Carroll

ISBN1-888842-38-5

Cover art: *The Art Student*, by Irving Amen. Reprinted by permission of the Hillel Jewish Center, Cinncinati, Ohio.

Designed by Edward E. Wilson

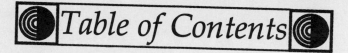

# Table of Contents

# Preface

All I am doing is pointing.
You must find it true for
yourself.

—The Buddha

Let's face it, you live in a world where entire wars are described in sound bites; you eat fast food, watch instant replays, and send e-mails. Yet as writers you are expected to develop your thoughts through writing. Readers want writing to be coherent, interesting, and have voice. They want layers of thought to dig into, but they don't want to get bogged down by words. So the dilemma for contemporary writers is how to avoid superficiality yet achieve depth.

You understand that writing is thought on paper and coherence, focus, and voice show depth of thought. Making that happen on the page isn't easy. Writing is hard work. Hemingway said it best, "Writing is easy. You just sit at the typewriter and bleed." Yet adding more, developing more, thinking ahead so the piece sticks together as if glued — one sentence to the next — one paragraph to the next — must seem as though you are being asked to open an old wound to let it bleed again.

It doesn't have to be that way. I like what Higgins advises,

> *You can get what you need to write (as opposed to what you need to make a big nuisance of yourself at cocktail parties) by shutting yourself in a room by yourself for twenty minutes a day and reading aloud from E. B. White's "Charlotte's Web" and going on from that to other works of skill, until you begin to see, by hearing, how much the choice and arrangement of the words contribute to the impact of the story, even when no sound is uttered in its reading. And you will begin to see, very quickly —*

*guaranteed (Winokur, 139).*
You'll read this advice as a recurring refrain many times in this book.

My intention is to provide a guide to depth—not Charles Dickens stuff—nothing antediluvian, archaic, uncool—but a guide into apt, clear, and lively writing. I invite you to take these suggestions and run with them.

So this guide offers proven strategies that promote layered thought in its first chapter—that is connecting thought with thought with thought in coherent and meaningful ways. The second chapter suggests ways to deepen writing. Chapter three deals with showing not telling, and four explores coherence, both internal and external, plus ways to "chain." The fifth chapter talks about voice; the sixth suggests a hands-on writer's checklist; the final chapter presents a thumbnail sketch of structure. But there are other things to consider—practicing, crafting, and the begging for inspiration.

Above all, though, know that when writing becomes challenging, interesting, and fun, not the rote following of some predetermined recipe, potential writers of all ages blossom into published writers. My hope is this book helps that happen for you. "All I am doing is pointing."

# Chapter 1
## The Strategies

Mastery is not something that strikes in an instant, like a thunderbolt, but a gathering power that moves steadily through time, like weather.

—John Gardner,
novelist & writing teacher

The strategies suggested in this chapter have been proven effective for all writers at all levels. Writers have adapted, altered, applied, modified, morphed, and expanded them to meet their needs. That is how it should be. You do the same. Here I offer the bare bones; you add the meat of your meaning. When you do, you'll achieve more depth, more interest, and more voice in your writing. But it takes time and lots and lots and lots of writing and reading and lots and lots and lots of patience and motivation, and lots and lots and lots of stick-to-itiveness.

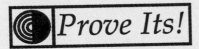

This is a sure-fire way to layer writing, and it's easy. Find relatively simple declarative sentences in your writing. They should not be the first or last sentences in your piece, nor should they be the first or last sentences in a paragraph. By underlining them in some color, they stand out.

These sentences are generally telling not showing sentences. Here are some examples:

> *The witch is ugly.*
> *My brother is mean.*
> *Our house is small.*
> *Work is boring.*
> *Johnny likes to run.*

You will notice each of these sentences simply tells something the reader is suppose to believe because the author wrote it. Think a chant after you reread each of your underlined sentences, "Maybe yes, maybe no. Prove it!" That chant gets fixed in the brain and reminds you to back up your statements. After that, choose one of your sentences and elaborate upon it. Something like:

> *The witch is ugly. Her stringy hair looks like the wet, dirty mop propped against the wall in my garage. Her snaggletooth grimace reveals a thin slimy green film and several missing teeth. She has a huge carbuncle on her left cheek with a long gray hair growing out of it. Her chin is pointy and hairy, her nose is bumpy and snotty, and her neck looks like limp crêpe paper.*

Notice how these sensory images set up a picture of the witch. Creating such an image allows the reader to see the witch as the writer sees her—not just accept *ugly* on the writer's word. Of course, every telling sentence doesn't demand elaboration, but when you read as writers and write as readers, you begin to develop a sense of when and where to do that layering. First, you must practice.

Have plenty of Post-its® handy. Challenge yourself to write a sentence or two on each of three or so Post-its® and place them one under the other on the page beneath your underlined sentence. This reinforces in your brain the notion of layered thought that will eventually become internalized. ("The witch is ugly" sentence yielded five layers.) At this point you do not have to rewrite. Pat yourself on the back for elaborating. Tip: The more fun you make this, the more eagerly you will work at it again and again.

A fine example of layered thought in young adult liter-

ature comes from *Harry Potter and the Sorcerer's Stone* where
Harry and Ron come upon the troll:

> *Harry sniffed and a foul stench reached his nostrils, a mixture of old socks and the kind of public toilet no one seems to clean.*
>
> *And then they heard it — a low grunting, and the shuffling footfalls of gigantic feet. Ron pointed — at the end of the passage to the left, something huge was moving toward them. They shrank into the shadows and watched as it emerged into a patch of moonlight.*
>
> *It was a horrible sight. Twelve feet tall, its skin was a dull, granite gray, its great lumpy body like a boulder with its small bald head perched on top like a coconut. It had short legs thick as tree trunks with flat, horny feet. The smell coming from it was incredible. It was holding a huge wooden club, which dragged along the floor because its arms were so long.*
>
> *The troll stopped next to a doorway and peered inside. It waggled its long ears, making up its tiny mind, then slouched slowly into the room.* (174)

Several paragraphs filled with sensory details (*great lumpy body, skin a dull, granite gray,*) odors (*a mixture of old socks and the kind of public toilet no one seems to clean,*) sounds (*low grunting, shuffling footfalls*), what they see (*waggled its long ears*), similes (*small bald head perched on top like a coconut, short legs thick as tree trunks*), vivid verbs (*sniffed, shrank, emerged, perched*), all paint an in-depth picture.

APPLICATION: Practice using *Harry* as a model. Place

yourself someplace unfamiliar, perhaps with a friend, and create something frightening. Write what happens. Share.

> WHAT HAVE YOU LEARNED
>   Rereading and reflection
>   Decision making
>   Declarative sentences
>   Showing not telling
>   Sensory imagery/Details
>   Layering thought
>   Showing depth of thinking
>   Oral reading and sharing

 *Depth Charging*

This strategy is a blood relative to *Prove Its!* Again begin by underlining in color a declarative sentence. Then ascertain the most interesting word, phrase, or clause in that sentence and circle it in color. (Kids, no matter how young, never circle *the, an, a,* or *to be* verbs.) On a Post-it®, write a sentence about what you circled. Make certain your new sentence connects to the original sentence. Then circle something in the new sentence and write out of what you circled. Repeat this two or three or four times, always checking your connections.

Again practice, practice, practice. A depth charge may look like this:

> *Once I won a Toni doll. (Circle doll.) Dolls were never my thing; I preferred reading or active games*

*like hopscotch. (Circle active.) Reading activated my mind, but games like hopscotch, jacks, and ball blocks kept me moving. (Circle moving.) With dolls you dressed them and mostly sat around with them. (Circle dolls.) So what was I going to do with a Toni doll?*

Sometimes first attempts are awkward, after all you are just getting the hang of this strategy, but eventually you will become proficient and your writing will be better for it.

As a test, read the section in your writing with the depth charging and without it. Reflect on the difference. Sometimes you'll need a transition or some sentence combining, but as you catch on, depth charging leads to a more fully developed paper.

In *Esperanza Rising* by Pam Muñoz Ryan, there is an excellent example of how depth charging looks in literature. The chapter is called "Las Uvas" or "Grapes." In this passage, Esperanza's parents, Ramona and Sixto Ortega, wealthy ranchers, are about to harvest their grapes. Sixto presents Esperanza with the knife and the honor of cutting the first cluster.

*...He [Papa] swept his hand toward the grapevines, signaling Esperanza. (Circle grapevines.) When she walked toward the arbors and glanced back at her parents, they both smiled and nodded, encouraging her forward. (Circle arbors.) When she reached the vines, she separated the leaves and carefully grasped a thick stem. (Circle thick stem.) She put the knife to it, and with a quick swipe, the heavy cluster of grapes dropped*

*into her waiting hand. (Circle heavy cluster of grapes.) Esperanza walked back to Papa and handed him the fruit. (Circle fruit.)*

Now Ryan concludes this passage.

*Papa kissed it and held it up for all to see.*

That concluding sentence ties the paragraph together with a coherent bow.

APPLICATION: Practice using *Esperanza Rising* as a model. Think about a time when you did something physical such as cleaning a closet or washing the car. Write about that using the depth charging strategy. Share.

> WHAT HAVE YOU LEARNED
>     Rereading and reflection
>     Decision making
>     Declarative sentences
>     Lexical choice
>     Coherence
>     Oral reading and sharing
>     Transitions
>     Sentence combining
>     Layering thought

# *Thought Bubbles*

This little goody comes from Barry Lane but is adapted here with a twist. Think about cartoons and how cartoonists show thought. Grab those Post-its® (I warned you to have plenty) and cut a few to look like the thought bubbles you see in comics. Amazingly, your bubbles will take on unique, individual qualities that reinforce the uniqueness and individuality of your writing. Reread your piece, choosing a place where a character (or the author, depending upon the nature of the writing) might do some thinking. Insert your Post-it® bubble at that spot and write the thought on the bubble.

Your process might go like this. You read a section of your writing:

> *My father and I used to go to the swamps in August to pick those great big blueberries called swamp berries. But he never let me go in where the berries grew biggest, so he always spilled some of his into my pail because he didn't let me in too far.*

I think I'll put my thought bubble after *far* because I remember wondering why he didn't allow me in too far. I remember asking him. I remember his answer.

He told me a story about how he'd go swamp berry picking with his buddies when he was my age. It went something like this: *"One day while we were goofing around, Milton fell into quicksand, and it sucked him down. It took all of us, holding and pulling on a big stick like a life and death tug-of-war, to drag him out. We were scared. I still hold that fear inside me. Son, I'm afraid if you got caught in quicksand, I wouldn't be able to pull you out."*

Wow! If I wrote that on my thought bubble, it would make those first two sentences better.

This is a good strategy to use in tandem with literature as authors do this all the time. Kate Di Camillo, in her award-winning book *Because of Winn-Dixie*, writes a thought bubble right off in Chapter One. India Opal Buloni, who was sent by her daddy to the Winn-Dixie grocery, witnesses a ruckus over a dog that has strayed into the store. Everyone is frantic to get the dog out, but Opal is afraid the dog, if caught, will be sent to the pound, so she calls the dog twice, "Here, boy..." Then comes the thought bubble:

> *And then I figured that the dog was probably just like everybody else in the world, that he would want to get called by a name, only I didn't know what his name was, so I just said the first thing that came into my head. I said, "Here, Winn-Dixie."*

That thought bubble gives the reader a great deal of information. We get insight into Opal, her sensitivity, her thinking process, and her cleverness. All that happens because of one thought bubble.

APPLICATION: Reenter your writing, reread, add thought bubbles in appropriate places, then fill them with "thinking writing." Share.

---

WHAT HAVE YOU LEARNED
  Rereading and reflection
  Decision making
  Extending a piece
  Anecdotes
  Oral reading and sharing
  Writing thought
  Elaboration
  A device to show a character's thoughts

Think of a lamp sitting on a desk in the dark, unplugged. You make your way over to it, fumble with the switch, nothing happens. You find the cord to the plug, feel around for the socket, and plug it in. Light! Now you can SEE. That is exactly what happens when you use this strategy. You find a simple sentence, a statement (S) (plug). Using the analogy of the cord, you extend that statement by restating it or by giving more information (E) (cord). Finally, you elaborate by putting the plug in the socket and lighting up the meaning (E) (lamp). When a statement has been written, extended, and elaborated, readers *see* the meaning; they comprehend, they understand. Layering makes writing strong. Conversely, when writing is not layered, it tends to be weak or superficial, often lacking important information.

A model from Seymour Simon's book *Sharks* illustrates SEE:

> *Probably the best known of all sharks is the great white shark. (S) It is the third largest shark, but the most dangerous. (E) In the movie Jaws, the great white was pictured as a fierce, intelligent, and unpredictable human-eating monster. But "human biting" is probably more accurate, because only rarely does a great white – or any other shark – actually eat people. (E)*

APPLICATION: Find or write your topic sentence. Extend and elaborate upon that sentence. You might want to share the results of this strategy with a small group and invite feedback. After SEE, listeners should have a clear idea of your intent. This is a particularly good strategy to use with non-fiction, expository prose, research, or topical essays and paragraphs.

> WHAT HAVE YOU LEARNED
>     Topic sentences
>     Supporting details
>     Extending topic sentences
>     Elaborating topic sentences
>     Listening skills
>     Clarity of expression
>     Group reflection
>     Sharing

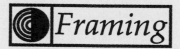 *Framing*

Why do we frame pictures of loved ones, special events, not-so-special events, things, animals, birds, butterflies, places? Look at your framed pictures and think about why you went through the trouble and expense of framing them—because you want to remember what's in the picture—because the picture is special. Perhaps you want to show the picture off to others. Somehow, by putting a frame around it, you proclaim, "Look, look at this!" Framing in writing also does that. It invites the reader to look at something closely.

This type of layering is everywhere in literature. The opening chapter "Silent Pictures" in Ann-Marie MacDonald's best selling novel, *Fall on Your Knees*, offers readers a series of pictures: of the town, street, house, and characters. We feel as if we are sitting with MacDonald as she turns album pages, sets up the context, gives us the background for what is to come:

> *Here's a picture of her* [Mumma] *the day she died. She had a stroke while cleaning the oven. Which is how the doctor put it. Of course you can't see her face for the oven, but you can see where she had her stockings rolled down for housework and, although this is a black and white picture, her housedress actually is black since she was in mourning for Kathleen at the time, as well as Ambrose. You can't tell from this picture, but Mumma couldn't speak English very well. Mercedes found her like that, half in half out of the oven like the witch in Hansel and Gretel. What did she plan to cook that day? When Mumma died, all the eggs in the pantry went bad—they must have because you could smell that sulphur smell all the way down Water Street.* (9-10)

At this point we don't know Mumma, Kathleen, Ambrose, or Mercedes, but we get a clear, framed picture in our minds. The added bonus of the "Hansel and Gretel" allusion adds another layer since it evokes all the darkness of that fairy tale. The reader gets not only abbreviated details about the stockings, the housedress, the mourning, some names, but also a close-up of Mumma half in and half out of the oven. What a picture! That's what framing does.

APPLICATION: Find a person, place, thing, animal, or event in your writing. Draw a box around it. Take a Post-it®, cut out a bit of its center to make a wide frame. Affix the frame over the box and write more on the frame. Try a detail that conveys the character of what is framed: a hairline crack in the antique vase, the thumb caught in the pocket of the teenager standing at a jaunty angle, the smile lines around grandmother's face, one board swinging by a nail at the old farmhouse, or an action that has been stilled forever.

This is another good time to share either in small groups or with a writer friend. Talk about the value of being specific and how writers notice the flickers in life.

---

WHAT HAVE YOU LEARNED
    Rereading and reflection
    Choice
    Specificity
    Characterization
        (things can have character;
          my dog has character)
    Details,
        (the close-ups that reveal deeper meanings)
    Sharing
    Evaluating

# ◉ *Café Squidd*

When entering a café, the customer usually gets a menu from which to pick and choose the fare. Café Squidd invites you to do the same. You know you can't eat everything on the menu, so you choose what you want. It's like that in writing. We choose what we do best. This is not a bad thing. We all enjoy what we do well and avoid what we do poorly. To grow as writers you should eventually sample all the fare to find your style and voice. This strategy promotes that sampling.

APPLICATION: Find a large piece of colored paper — construction paper will do. Remember the brain associates color with what is being learned or attempted. Fold the sheet in half to resemble a menu. On the cover write "Café Squidd" and your name, which reinforces ownership.

Inside on the left-hand side, write in large script the letters **C-A-F-É** vertically down the page. On the right-hand side, write the letters **S Q U I D D**. Now all is ready.

Next to each letter, write the technique that letter represents. Find an example of that technique in your reading. Decide if you want to add that technique to your writing. Remember: Choice is important.

C **Comparisons** — something is like something else — similes, metaphors, or simply looking at one thing and seeing another.

A **Anecdotes**—little stories—the parts of a narrative, noticing dramatic moments, pulling the drama out of an experience.

F **Facts**—the *act* in *fact*— what it means to have "actual existence," an actual occurrence that can be verified.

E **Examples**—think: *for example, for instance* as an additional way to clarify meaning.

S **Statistics**—numbers or data to prove something— estimates, reasonable answers, charts, responses, polls, graphs, surveys, tables, ratio.

QU—**Quotations**—something said by someone else, by someone famous or knowledgeable in a discipline— credibility, resources for quotations, saving favorite quotations, connecting quotations to the text, integrating quotations within the writing.

I **Illustrations**—words that make pictures in the mind- —imagery, using the senses to create pictures.

D **Details**—close-ups, specifics, what you would see if you were only five inches away, the close-ups taken by a camera or video.

D **Descriptions**—long shots—general characteristics of a thing, what you would see if you were several feet away or looking from a distance, the long shots taken by a camera or video.

---

WHAT HAVE YOU LEARNED
  Figurative language
  Narration as elaboration
  Supporting details
  Generalizations
  Quantifiable data

> Testimony
> Propaganda devices
> Imagery
> Choice
> Creativity

# ⊚ *Starring*

This strategy uses the classic nursery rhyme "Twinkle Twinkle" as a foundation for its mnemonic. Review the words:

> *Twinkle, twinkle*
> *Little star*
> *How I wonder what you are*
> *Up above the sky so high*
> *Like a diamond in the sky.*

The first line repeats, reminding you to use repetition; the second names, reminding you to name, rename, or be specific; the third line invites conjecture and prediction or description and explanation; the fourth sets the context or setting, and the fifth suggests similes or comparisons.

APPLICATION: Make a five-pointed star. Write *repetition* on one point of your star, *specificity* on the next, *description/explanation/conjecture/prediction* on the third, *context/setting* on the fourth, and *similes/comparisons* on the last point. Write the title of your work in the middle (even if it is a working title). Then literally move your star over your paper as you reread each sentence. If you think you could add one of the points somewhere, do it. It will illuminate your writing.

Sharon Creech's *A Fine, Fine School* shows the power of these points. The use of the repetitive word *fine* runs throughout the book as a fine, fine example of effective repetition. Throughout the book, Creech uses the characters' specific names: *Mr. Keene*, the principal; *Beans*,the dog; *Tillie*, the main character. While the illustrations offer description, as is the way in children's books, Mr. Keene explains:

> *We will learn all about numbers and letters, colors*
> *and shapes, the Romans and the Egyptians and the*
> *Greeks. We will learn about dinosaurs and castles*
> *and – and – everything!*

Then he repeats for emphasis,

> *We will learn everything!*

Throughout the book, Creech provides context and setting: the hallway, classes, where Tille lives, the bus, the tree, the days of the week, the time of the year, and, of course, the *fine, fine school.*

Comparisons abound: the difference between Tillie and her brother, what they do during the week compared to what they do on weekends, the way the principal perceives the school and the way the teachers and students perceive it, what Tillie does on Christmas and what Beans and her brother do, and so on. This is a fine, fine book to consult for starring.

| WHAT HAVE YOU LEARNED |
| --- |
| Rhetorical choice |
| Specificity |
| Description |
| Explanation |

> Meaningful context
> Setting
> Apt similes and/or comparisons
> Effective repetition

# ◉ *Tampering with Time*

Don't you wish you could tamper with time — stretch it when you need to reflect or when you are having fun, but squeeze it when things become boring or unbearable? As an author, you can do that. You are powerful, so powerful you can control time by expanding it when it needs to be expanded — hence, deepening the writing — or condensing what could be or is boring. This is called *pacing* in theater and *timing* in sports. Actors with a sense of pacing hold the audience because they know when to speed things up and when to linger in the moment. Athletes with timing know when to jump, turn, pause, risk, stop. They often enjoy greatness because of this.

You, too, must develop this sense. Writing on and on about some minute detail may bore or illuminate, yet giving just the right amount of time to an incident or an anecdote may cause the reader to experience eureka. Only through writing, writing, writing — the practice of the craft, does this sense become art.

Find a place in your writing that indicates time. This could be as obvious as a specific date, *December 12*, or as

subtle as *when I was little*. Circle your choice, slap a Post-it®
there and go on to expand that time. Likewise, reread to
check if you have already written too much, or if you
should tightened for dramatic effect. In a crazy kind of
way, sometimes knowing what to do is based on knowing
what not to do. Too much can lengthen a piece to tedium;
not enough thins the writing, makes it so superficial it lacks
substance or meaning and leaves the reader unsatisfied.

Watch a video clip of some actor, Charlie Chaplin in the
famous *The Gold Rush* "dancing rolls" sequence, or view a
rerun from the Olympics where the skaters or skiers exhib-
it their impeccable sense of timing. Analyze the timing.

In *The Tortilla Curtain*, T.C. Boyle stretches time so taut-
ly we feel what the character feels. In the following excerpt,
Candido has taken his pregnant wife America to Canoga
Park to find an apartment. They are illegal aliens and have
been living in the desert trying to work and save. A man
approaches Candido, offers him a place to stay—cheap—
but insists he go with him to look at the place. Candido tells
America to wait. The reader screams, "Don't go, Candido;
it's a scam."

> *The first fifteen minutes were nothing. America
> never asked herself what she was doing sitting on
> that concrete wall out front of the post office build-
> ing in Canoga Park, never gave it a thought. She
> was exhausted, her feet ached, she felt hot and
> sleepy and a little nauseous, and she just sat there
> in a kind of trance and let the rich stew of the city
> simmer around her....*

Two paragraphs later:

> *The second fifteen minutes were no problem either,*
> *though there was more of an edge to them, a hard*
> *hot little prick of anxiety that underscored the pass-*
> *ing of each separate sixty-second interval. Where is*
> *Candido?...*

The next paragraph begins:

> *There was a clock in the window of the appliance-*
> *repair shop across the way, and as the big illumi-*
> *nated pointer began to intrude on the third quarter*
> *of the hour, she realized that her nausea had begun*
> *to feature the brief powerful constrictions of*
> *hunger....*

So now Boyle places this illegal alien, this pregnant woman we have come to care about, alone in a city. Her husband has already been gone too long and she is tired and hungry. The next paragraph starts:

> *During the final quarter hour a man in stained*
> *clothes appeared out of nowhere and sat beside her*
> *on the wall....*
>
> *Then it was the second hour and she was lost and*
> *abandoned....*

In this paragraph, America begins to question Candido's intentions, then worries he had an accident, had a heart attack, then fears he has been picked up by *La Migra*. Finally she realizes her own predicament.

> *After an hour and a half had gone by and there was*
> *still no sign of him, America pushed herself up from*
> *the wall...*

and she begins to search for him.

*It was getting dark*

She is frightened, exhausted to the point that she nods off close to midnight. Candido finally returns. As feared by the reader, he has been beaten and robbed (230-234).

So craftily does Boyle write this sequence that we sit on the wall, we stare at the clock, we are frightened, we worry, we realize our predicament. So craftily does Boyle elongate time, that when we finish reading, we feel like Salvador Dali's watch hanging limply over the naked branch in *The Persistence of Memory*.

APPLICATION: Try writing a passage using this excerpt from Boyle as a model. Scour literature for other examples of time tampering. Think about what the tampering does to the meaning and to the depth.

---

WHAT HAVE YOU LEARNED

Reading and writing are flip sides of the same coin

Layering as a technique can be used to manipulate time

Ways to develop a sense of timing when writing

Rereading

Reading literature to enhance writing

Writing to create literature

Choice

Connecting writing to other arts and to sports

# *Hexagonal Writing*
## RESPONDING IN DEPTH TO LITERATURE

Don't think about responding to literature as merely retelling the plot. That hardly shows depth of thought. I can say, "Romeo and Juliet were in love" without understanding motivation or intensity, without knowing the intricacies of social strictures, without knowing anything about the era. Likewise, someone can write, "Cinderella had a fairy godmother" but fail to connect that character to literary devices such as the sophisticated *deus ex machina*. So, what to do? What strategy will encourage you to expand your repertoire of response and deepen your understanding? I have developed hexagonal writing as a way to do that. It is a six-part heuristic that begins simply and ends with higher level thinking. Here's how it works.

The first step in writing with depth about literature is to read the work analytically. This means not only are you expected to read and comprehend, but you are also expected to develop ideas about the information contained in the work as you read.

Hexagonal writing is structured to enhance analytic reading thereby creating the habit of thought (Strong, 35).

Take any piece of literature (narrative works best at first). Write the plot summary—something you probably would do quite naturally. Then make a connection between something in your life or experience and that piece of literature. After doing this, figure out the message in the piece, its theme, why the author even bothered to write it. Next, reenter the piece to ferret out its literary devices, connecting these devices to the message/theme. Following that (you can see the difficulty increasing with each step), connect the piece of literature to some other piece of literature or to some social event, film, song—something outside yourself. Finally, evaluate the piece by taking a stand about it and using textual references from the piece to support what you think. By this time you have enough prewriting to develop a well-elaborated literary analysis. Plot, personal associations, theme, analysis, literary allusions, evaluation—render the analysis complete, only the trimmings need to be added. Organize the six parts in a way that logically and cohesively hangs everything together, add some transitions, and maybe rework the lead.

APPLICATION: Choose a short story or narrative poem and orally work through the heuristic. You may want to apply this strategy to your own writing. Using it this way becomes a self evaluative tool to find the holes, spaces, blurs, tangles in your writing.

---

WHAT HAVE YOU LEARNED
    Close reading and rereading
    Literary analysis
    Appropriate elaboration
    Literary connections
    Plot summary
    Personal allusions
    Theme
    Analysis

Literary devices appropriate to the genre
Literary allusions
Evaluation of a literary work
Comparisons of literary papers
Structure of a paper
Transitions needed to help meaning
Textual references
Leads
Logic
Coherence

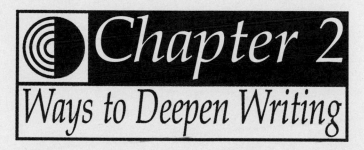

# Chapter 2
# Ways to Deepen Writing

*Fear is at the root of most bad writing.*

—Stephen King,
novelist

If you write daily, you don't fear writing. You have chosen to embark on a journey to gain confidence, uncover voice and style. But you know that honing figurative language and crafting your writing makes it better. The suggestions in this chapter capture the natural ways writers write and are offered here with examples and applications so that they will become natural for you—but, again, each takes practice. And make no mistake, these devices are not only for adult writers. Nothing could be further from the truth. Children use most of these devices when they write and speak—they just don't use the literary terms, nor could they tell you the literary term they are using.

Once in my studies, a teacher explained that everything we study as literary terminology was first a natural outgrowth of perception. As people became more sophisticated, they assigned names to these natural processes thereby codifying them. She used *personification* as her example. She hypothesized a story about someone walking in the forest at night, long before electricity was discovered, when the trees were dark outlines against the moonlit sky. That early poet noticed how the tree branches looked like arms lifted to the sky, how the trunk of the tree seemed like a person's body. There, she said, on that night, the notion of personification was born.

So think of these as natural processes; don't make these terms intimidating. Learn them. Practice them. Internalize them. Take risks with them.

In truth, all literary devices may be used to elaborate. Although stringing adjectives along the way to a noun might constitute sentence expansion, that is horizontal not vertical elaboration, not depth of thought. Honing literary devices goes a long way to develop writers.

ALLUSION is simply a reference to another person, place, thing, event, or literary work. It can be explicit by actually naming the referent,

> *She works like the third little pig in the folktale –*
> *industriously, cleverly, and smart.*

Or an allusion may be implicit,

> *He belongs in a fairy tale not sitting next to me in*
> *English class, a fairy tale where little girls would*
> *not notice how conniving he was.*

The beauty of allusion is that it enlarges and enhances the subject because when we get it, our minds naturally supply the information from the allusion to the text where it has been added.

Toni Morrison, winner of the Nobel Prize in Literature, begins her novel *The Bluest Eye* with a telling allusion, one referring to the once ubiquitous Scott Foresman reading series "Dick and Jane." The first page is all Pollyanna with a pretty house, happy children, a secure family, and friends. On the second page, Morrison plays with the language found on page one, mixing it up, confusing it, and finally running all the words together for eleven lines. In two pages, with that economy of language allusion provides, we understand. Clearly Morrison tells the reader, this will be no "Dick and Jane" story.

APPLICATION: Choose an event you remember, for example your high school prom or something that tugged at you then or tugs still.

> *I was Cinderella, but he certainly proved to be no Prince Charming!*
>
> *When I first moved, I felt like the Beast. I was an outsider. I didn't know the school, and I didn't have any friends, and I sure didn't have a Beauty.*

The trick is to use allusion wisely and well in your writing; use it with security and purpose.

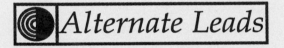

# Alternate Leads

LEADS are generally considered the first two sentences or so of a work. Writing alternative leads to experiment with better hooks often may be incorporated into the writing for added depth. By challenging yourself to write alternative leads (other than "I am going to tell you about...") using action, reaction, dialogue, glimpses of character, setting (other than "one sunny day"), you will probably write two, four, or ten more sentences on those Post-its®, creating what I call "post-a-notes possibilities."

After doing this exercise several times myself, I realized that after I chose the best lead, those other Post-it® leads could be salvaged. I noodled around with them and discovered how easily I could add one or more of them to my introductions or beginnings. (We all know how writers hate to throw away anything they have written.) In fact, once you prioritize your leads, you, too, will realize that the "post-a-note possibilities" often beg to become extensions or restatements. In most cases neophyte writers are delighted to discover they don't have to trash anything. In all cases, this salvaging adds layers to your first, off-the-tip-of-the-pen, often mundane, predictable lead. Here is what happened to one writer:

Her original typical, ho hum lead:

> *One day we decided to go to Mexico to eat Mexican food. There were three of us.*

This throat-clearing lead got her started but it's right up there with "One dark and stormy night..."

1st try using reaction:

> *A tingle always runs down my spine as I cross the border from the United States to Mexico. I think it is born of a sense of adventure, a sense of mystery.*

2nd try using dialogue:

> *"Let's go across the border to eat Mexican food," Dad suggested. "You and Mom can go shopping."*

3rd try using action:

> *We neared the booth of the uniformed border guards – a family of three frantically fetching coins out of their pockets to pay the toll. Dad found two quarters, Mom gave him two more, and I handed him my two just in time. He passed the change to the guard, and we were on our way to Reynosa.*

Because each lead is on a separate Post-it®, you may rearrange and manipulate them to see if they make sense rearranged differently, if they stuck together, if they add

new or more specific information, or if they work to draw
the reader into the piece. Most of the time, writers keep all
their leads. In the case above, the writer made the following decisions:

1. She thought beginning with dialogue sounded the
best. "That's the way it happened," she said.

2. She decided to put her third try next, followed by try
number one.

3. She chose to trash her ho hum lead completely saying,
"I already gave that information in a more interesting way.

So her throat-clearing lead evolved into this:

> *"Let's go across the border to eat Mexican food,"*
> *Dad suggested. "You and Mom can go shopping."*
>
> *We neared the booth of the uniformed border*
> *guards — a family of three frantically fetching coins*
> *out of their pockets to pay the toll. Dad found two*
> *quarters, Mom gave him two more, and I handed*
> *him my two just in time. He passed the change to*
> *the guard, and we were on our way to Reynosa. A*
> *tingle always runs down my spine as I cross the*
> *border from the United States to Mexico. I think it*
> *is born of a sense of adventure, a sense of mystery.*

As you can see, this opener is more coherent; it does,
indeed, hook the reader and the added depth, which was
inside the writer all the time, happened painlessly. The
"post-a-notes possibilities" are non-threatening, but when
completed offer more information by layering your
thoughts. (For a complete list of possible leads, see
Appendix A.)

APPLICATION: Challenge yourself to write two or three

alternative leads to one of your writings. Then noodle with them to see what happens.

# ⊚ *Anecdote*

ANECDOTE is nothing more than a "little story" or single incident nestled inside a larger work often to make a point or to draw a comparison between component parts in the piece.

My mother was a master of the anecdote. When she would admonish me not to do something, "Don't put your fingers in the washing machine's wringer!" she would inevitably follow up with an anecdote. "I know a little girl who didn't listen to her mother. She got her whole hand so stuck, she couldn't pull it out. Her parents had to call the ambulance. They had to pry open the wringers. Her hand was crushed, so they took her to the hospital." Mom might even add — depending upon how emphatically she wanted to make her point — something ghoulish — "and they had to cut off all her fingers!"

I chuckle now as I look back on her motherly child psychology, but I know I remember the warning more because of the story than by the admonishment.

Story used this way is called *exemplum* and was popularized by preachers in the Middle Ages. Chaucer, in *The Pardoner's Tale*, wrote a story of three revelers who set out to find Death but found gold instead. They kill each other for the gold, which underscores the Pardoner's message,

"Greed is the root of all evil." Incidentally, the German folktale *The Musicians of Bremen*, retold most recently by Jane Yolen, is an adaptation of Chaucer's tale as is the 1947 Humphrey Bogart, Walter Huston film *The Treasure of Sierra Madre*. Obviously anecdotes hold the promise of larger works.

APPLICATION: Take an anecdote from one of your writings. Try to work up your "little story" into a longer piece. Reread your work. Or try to find a place where adding a "little story" in your writing would make your point.

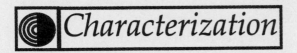

# Characterization

CHARACTERIZATION is hyped description that distinguishes a character in some way meaningful to the story. Long detailed descriptions of characters tend to bore the reader—better to illuminate them through action, dialogue, a few choice details.

We refer to characters as *flat* or *round*. Flat characters become comic or stereotypic. Both insult the reader. Although sometimes flat characters are needed much the way walk-on actors provide background in a street scene for a movie or TV show, the major and minor characters need to be rounded out. They need to display the complexity, surprise, and the motivations of real people.

To achieve a round character, create a memory jogger. Get a cheap (the cheapest you can find) paper pie plate. Fold it in half, in half again, and in half a third time. You will have eight sections. Label each section in the fluted part: *name, description, inner qualities, actions, dialogue, impact, comparisons, reaction.* Use it on yourself.

Then choose a character from a piece if literature rich with characters and systematically fill in all the *names* of the character, nick names, pet names, and other names in the "filling" portion of the plate. For *description,* list the physical qualities of the character. In the space *inner qualities,* jot personality traits, mannerisms, beliefs. For *actions,* record verbs that fit the character. Under *dialogue,* pick some dialogue spoken by the character that is revelatory or significant. If the character does not speak, write what you think the character would say. *Impact* invites you to analyze how the character influences one or several other characters. Try various *comparisons* to birds, animals, or things to shift your writing angle so that you open up, tinkering with the character in different ways. Record your *reactions,* your feelings and thoughts about the character. A good way to get at this is to ask, "Would I want to be friends with this character?"

APPLICATION: Once you have done this about yourself and a literary character, use this pie plate nudge for developing characters in your own writing. Rounding out characters enables an important and deep level of insight into the human condition — even for young writers.

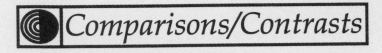

# Comparisons/Contrasts

In rhetorical parlance, this device is sometimes called THESIS/ANTITHESIS and is different from similes or metaphors. Here we look more at the grammatical structure, often the parallelism where a statement is made and then is followed by a syntactical parallel that stands in opposition.

An example from Samuel Johnson's *Rasselas*, Chapter 26:

> *"Marriage has many pains, but celibacy has no pleasures."*

We find thesis/antithesis in academic writing, "We do not need to focus on 'voice' but on having something to say." The word *but* sets up the contrast. Children use this device all the time, "I'll play Barbie with you, but you have to play Pokémon with me." Or, "I'll go bed, but first read me a story."

For a quick study of thesis/antithesis turn to Judith Viorst. *Alexander and the Terrible, Horrible, No Good, Very Bad Day* is replete with them. Viorst's story illustrates how well writing can be elaborated by using one technique. While Viorst doesn't always explicitly use the word *but*, it is implied because the thesis and its opposite are there.

The book begins,

> *I went to sleep with gum in my mouth* (THESIS) *and now there's gum in my hair...*(ANTITHESIS).

Nick finds a code ring in his breakfast cereal box, (THESIS) but Alexander only finds breakfast cereal (ANTITHESIS). Dad tells him not to fool around with his phone (THESIS), but Alexander thinks he called Australia (ANTITHESIS).

> *They made me buy plain old white ones* [sneakers] *(THESIS), but they can't make me wear them (antithesis).*

APPLICATION: Try this sophisticated yet not difficult (see there it is again) literary device. Try comparisons and contrasts in your writing. Often thesis/antithesis produces a side effect: It's easy to continue to write because you have already set up tension. Tension strengthens the writing that follows. As the oatmeal commercial advises, "Try it. It's the right thing to do."

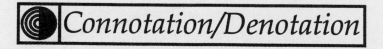

# Connotation/Denotation

I know, I know, you don't see how CONNOTATION and DENOTATION can be part of developing depth in writing, but they are. Using a word that is unusual but appropriate in the context of writing often begs for a definition. I am fond of pointing to E. B. White's work (He's the sidekick of Strunk, incidentally.) as a model. In *Charlotte's Web*, White writes the following exchange between the curious Wilbur and the savvy Charlotte:

> "I was just thinking," said the spider, "that people are very gullible."
> "What does 'gullible' mean?"

*"Easy to fool," said Charlotte.* (67)

Notice how by simply supplying the definition or the denotation of the word, White expands that section while simultaneously giving the reader a glimpse into the characters. In a real sense, definition illuminates diction (word choice) and diction illuminates definition. Working with words, using dictionary/thesaurus skills, you can easily weave words into a piece for added depth. Sometimes denotation is called *referential* or *cognitive* language because it is matter-of-fact.

E.B White plays with the connotation of words equally well. Again, a passage from *Charlotte's Web*:

> *"...But no — with men it's rush, rush, rush, every minute. I'm glad I'm a sedentary spider."*
>
> *"What does sedentary mean?" asked Wilbur.*
>
> *"Means I sit still a good part of the time and don't go wandering all over creation. I know a good thing when I see it, and my web is a good thing. I stay put and wait for what comes. Gives me a chance to think."* (61)

Here White provides a range of secondary or accompanying meanings, associations, nuances; and, by extension, he invites the reader to participate by thinking, perhaps, how wonderful it must be to have a special place and not have to rush around. This language almost always creates a chain of associations. Because connotation often evokes feelings, it is sometimes called *emotive* language. Bring to your work the connotative as well as the denotative meaning of words. Fledglings can greatly enhance the depth of their writing, layer their thoughts, using connotation and denotation.

SMALL_CAPS: APPLICATION: Reread your work. Circle unusual words. Reenter by providing the denotations or connotations in the manner of E.B. White. Reflect upon what happens to your writing.

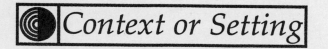

## Context or Setting

CONTEXT OR SETTING needs to be explored sans the gaggy "One summer day...One winter day...One dark and stormy night..." Setting, an important part of any work, establishes the locale and time in which the action occurs. To get a feel for setting, read and analyze many works in order to see how good writers create context without cliché. Also, as your reading and writing matures, you will come to see context or setting expand to include mood, ambiance, tone (attitude of the piece), the psychological or symbolic arena, even the mindset of characters.

Classics such as Shakespeare's *Macbeth* or Joyce's *Ulysses* show physical locations—Medieval Scotland in the former, Dublin, specifically June 16, 1904, in the latter. Stories by Poe, Kipling, Dickens read in tandem with contemporary works by Tan, Meyers, Yep, and nonfiction pieces both classic and modern, illuminate setting. Consider the setting in Charles Kuralt's essay, "Independence Hall."

> *"I say let us wait" John Dickinson of Pennsylvania*
> *stood in this hall, July 1st, 1776, and begged the*

*Continental Congress to be reasonable."* (604)
Ernesto Galarza delineates the setting differently in his personal essay, *Barrio Boy*:

> *My mother and I walked south on Fifth Street one morning to the corner of Q Street and turned right. Half of the block was occupied by the Lincoln School. It was a three-story wooden building, with two wings that gave it the shape of a double-T connected by a central hall. It was a new building, painted yellow, with a shingled roof that was not like the red tile of the school in Mazatlan. I noticed other differences, none of them very reassuring.*
> (611)

In one paragraph Galarza conveys not only the physical setting but also the psychological context. This is the first day of school for a boy who knows and comes from Mazatlan, the seaport in western Mexico. The last phrase gives the reader a glimpse into the anxieties of the character; the reader's context is expanded to include the narrator's.

Children's books are fine sources for context and setting. Precise and concise describe the setting for *An Amish Wedding* by Richard Ammon:

> *My sister Anna is getting married!*
> *In late spring when the strawberry patch was full of blossoms, Samuel asked her to be his wife.*

In *Leonardo's Horse* , author Jean Fritz lyrically lures the reader:

> *Anyone who watched the young Leonardo wander the countryside around his home in Vinci might*

*have guessed that he would be an artist. He stopped
to examine everything. He looked at the landscape
as if he were memorizing it. So it was no surprise
when his father took him as a young teenager to
Florence to study art.*

Byrd Baylor devotes her entire book *I'm in Charge of
Celebrations* to locale. Here is a sample:

> *Sometimes people ask me, "Aren't you lonely out
> there with just desert around you?" I guess they
> mean the beargrass and the yuccas and the cactus
> and the rocks. I guess they mean the deep ravines
> and the hawk nest in the cliffs and the coyote trails
> that wind across the hills.*

It doesn't get better than that for context, setting, and layering!

APPLICATION: Using the examples above as models,
rework or change the context and setting in one of your
writings. Try it. You'll like what it does.

# Description/Detail

DESCRIPTION provides the big picture, the background,
the long shot. It's like the opening sequence of *Citizen Kane*
by Orson Wells. In the background, Xanadu sits on a
mountaintop surrounded by a gate distinguished by the
letter "K." We see windows covered with ornate grillwork.
There is a moat, statues, a drawbridge, and a golf course in
disrepair. We get the context through these long shots.

Quickly, though, we experience a close-up, DETAILS of a snow-covered house with snowmen surrounding it. As the camera moves out from those details, we realize that the house and snowman are inside a globe. This sequence closes with an extreme close-up of Kane's lower face; we see every line, every curve. Then his lips whisper, "Rosebud."

Joyce Carol Oates in *We Were the Mulvaneys* superimposes setting and description, followed by exquisite details as Judd leaves the farmhouse one night to follow the deer:

> I crept up to the pond, which was only about three
> feet deep at this end....
>
> A single doe was drinking at the pond! I crouched
> in the grasses, watching from about fifteen feet
> away. I could see her long slender neck out-
> stretched. Her muzzle lowered to the water. By
> moonlight the doe was drained of color and on the
> pond's surface light moved in agitated ripples from
> where she drank...(21).

In the world of children's literature, we look to *Cook-a-doodle-doo!* by Janet Stevens and Susan Stevens Crummel. The book opens with a two-page spread. On the left side is a close-up of the head of a rooster; on the right side is a long shot of the barnyard. This scene shows a barn, two silos, a house, trees, furrows, a weather vane shaped like a rooster. The close-up shows the details—the closed eye of the rooster, his tongue. The point is that you can see the rooster weather vane as part of the big picture, but you can not see any specifics, any details. These come with the close-up.

APPLICATION: To further reinforce this distinction, take one index card. Punch a small hole in the card and pretend it is a camera. Find a place in the room and write what you see. Move closer. Look again through your "camera." Notice all the specific things you couldn't see from a distance. Capture what you see. Practice this often until you see the world with both eyes.

# Dialogue

DIALOGUE is a linguistic act engaging two parties. Multilogue is a linguistic act in which several people participate—one at a time—or sometimes, as is often the case in everyday conversation—all at once. You need to write both in natural ways that fit your writing.

Conversation should flow in an out of a piece like water from a faucet. Your chitchat should be different than a rap session, which must be different from pillow talk. A lecture shouldn't sound like a conference. These distinctions not only take careful crafting but also an ear for idiom, accent, word choice, and apt language. Remember language is apt when it fits the subject, the audience, and melts in with your voice and style. If something sounds out of place, it probably is.

When all the characters in a story sound like you, the dialogue or multilogue doesn't work. When characters speak in forced, stilted ways, the results can be comic. Remember: Writing is not transcribed speech. As Anne Lamott says,

> *Dialogue is the way to nail character, so you have to*

> *work on getting the voice right...You're not repro-*
> *ducing actual speech — you're translating the sound*
> *and rhythm of what a character says into words.*
> (67)

Incorporating dialogue or multilogue into your writing in apt ways at apt times does much to develop depth of character. Francisco Jiménez, in his book *Breaking Through*, uses dialogue to set up a poignant moment with his illiterate but loving mother. Miss Bell, his ninth grade English teacher, has made some suggestions on a paper he wrote about his younger brother. Eager to achieve, he sets about the task of correcting and revising:

> *As I retyped it on the kitchen table, Mama came over and sat next to me. "It's late, Panchito," she said softly. "Time for bed."*
>
> *"I am almost finished."*
>
> *"What are you working on, mijo?"*
>
> *"It's a paper I wrote for my English class on Trampita. My teacher liked it," I said proudly.*
>
> *"On Trampita!" she exclaimed.*
>
> *She got up and stood behind me. She placed her hands on my shoulders and asked me to read it. When I finished, I felt her tears on the back of my neck.* (99)

APPLICATION: Choose one of your writings. Find a place to add depth through dialogue. It doesn't have to be a long excerpt. Use Jiménez as exemplar.

# 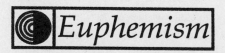*Dramatic Monologue/Soliloquy*

Both DRAMATIC MONOLOGUE and SOLILOQUY if employed with style can complete meaning and add depth.

The DRAMATIC MONOLOGUE is a technique, kin to dialogue, where a character, who is not the author, speaks at a critical moment. Sometimes, as in Judith Viorst's *The Good-Bye Book*, the person delivering the monologue addresses and even interacts with other people in the story, but we only hear the monologue and can only infer responses (this is a good exercise for inference as well). Dramatic monologue is an excellent technique to extend the temperament and motivation of a character.

SOLILOQUY is the act of talking to oneself as in Hamlet's "To be or not to be" speech, considered the best known of all soliloquies. It conveys the thinking of a character, especially in time of crisis to reveal a significant facet of the character's personality or motivation.

APPLICATION: Reenter your work. Decide if a character delivering a monologue or talking to him or herself would enhance it.

# *Euphemism*

EUPHEMISM, a word derived from the Greek, means *to*

*speak well.* Instead of bluntly saying something disagreeable, offensive, or terrifying, people use euphemisms to convey the same idea in a kinder, gentler way. This ability to soften an offensive expression offers another layer of thought.

All of which reminds me of an experience I had with some wonderful teachers from Mississippi. After three days of training, they graciously arranged a small dinner party for my husband and me. As we talked, I was struck with how melodious their language sounded compared to my brusque northeastern speech patterns. Finally, I couldn't contain myself any longer. "You all sound so pleasant when you speak. I do wish I could cultivate that characteristic and not sound so direct."

"Why, Honey," one of them drawled, "don't you know the trick?"

"Trick?"

"Why, yes. You just preface anything unpleasant with 'Bless your heart.' It works like this, 'Bless your heart, you are so fat!' or 'Bless your heart, your son is a slow learner.' That takes the edge off." And I had a lesson from a master of euphemism.

In everyday life, phrases such as *passed away* replace *died,* policemen no longer carry *clubs* but *night batons,* and the old distasteful *tax collector* has become the *revenue agent.*

Granted, euphemisms may add to the fun of manipulating language, but they do not always provide layer after layer of thought. Yet, depending upon how much the writer "talks around" an unpleasant topic, using euphemisms may be just the device needed. Take this example from *The New Yorker:*

*A man was hired by an oil company to take com-*
*plaints over the telephone. On his first day, he jot-*
*ted down a customer's complaint about an oil burn-*
*er that had exploded. It was his boss who then*
*exploded: You won't get far in this business until*
*you learn that we do not have explosions. We have*
*"PUFFBACKS".* (Espy, 49)

This perfect example shows how euphemisms may be
used to extend a piece.

APPLICATION: Have fun finding them: *light-fingered gen-*
*try* (thieves), *beauty cake* (bar of soap), *final resting place*
(cemetery), *pre-owned vehicles* (used cars). See what you discover about language and the mind. Have fun creating and
writing them.

# Euphony/Cacophony

EUPHONY is a fancy name for language that is easy on
the ears. Conversely, CACOPHONY is language that is harsh,
rough, or hard on the ears. The power of using euphony
and cacophony in writing is that both allow words to
match meaning. My favorite example of this match is the
family created by William Faulkner—the Snopes. When
you think of words beginning with SN, you generally think
of words like *sneer, snivel, sneaky, snake*—words that, even
coming through the nasal passage on the way to being spoken, create dissonance. On the other hand, e.e. cummings's
poem "in Just—" uses words to create feelings of happi-

ness, euphoria—*whistles far and wee*. Children's books, are filled with examples. Look no further than *The Three Billy Goats Gruff*—any version. All those guttural cacophonous GR sounds, *grass, ground, gruff, groaned* as well as the hard sound of G in *goat* prepares the reader for tough goats that will conquer the ugly troll.

Knowledge of phonics helps when writing because the sounds of our language are inextricably bound to meaning. Wanting to reinforce that concept, scholar Laurence Perrine titled his book on poetry *Sound and Sense*. Words that are higher on the scale such as *baby* and *whee* suggest euphonic meaning; words that are lower on the scale such as *boo hoo* and *broken* cause cacophony, especially if they are used, like cymbals, to clang against each other.

Reading aloud is important in the development of this technique. Read something like *Chicka Chicka Boom Boom!* by Bill Martin and John Archambault and think about what the sounds do to the poem's meaning. Read poems such as Poe's "The Bells" and notice the words he selected. Conjecture on why he chose them: *merriment, melody, tinkle, icy, oversprinkle, crystalline, tintinnabulation*. What is the effect of the repetitive use of the word *bells* seven times in a row?

Find collections of poetry to read aloud such as Pat Mora's *Confetti: Poems for Children*, or Ashley Bryan's *Sing to the Sun*, or Sandra DeCoteau Orie's *Did You Hear Wind Sing Your Name? An Oneida Song of Spring*, most anything by Jack Prelutsky or Shel Silverstein, or *Cool Salsa: Bilingual Poems on Growing Up Latino in the United States*, edited by Lori M. Carlson, or *Come With Me: Poems for a Journey* by

Naomi Shihab Nye, or *I Am the Darker Brother: An Anthology of Modern Poems by African Americans,* edited by Arnold Adoff, or *Poetry After Lunch: Poems to Read Aloud,* edited by Joyce Armstrong Carroll and Edward E. Wilson. Always there are words and sounds to think about; always they connect to meaning.

But don't exclude prose. The nonfiction story, "Harley Holladay: Black Sunday," about the dust storms in Phillip Hoose's *We Were There, Too! Young People in U.S. History* contains startling lines that flow and others that create dissonance.

> *We had hung the laundry out on the line...*

has an almost lullaby quality. We think of sheets flapping in the breeze, and we are lulled. But after the dust storms, Hoose chooses different language,

> *At the end of a workday their clothes were caked,*
> *their hair was matted, and their skin was streaked*
> *with dust.*

The hard *C* and the double plosive *T* along with the hiss of the fricative *S*, ending with a final plosive *T*, cause the reader to vicariously experience those black blizzards of soil that ripped across the land.

> *We want to spit out the grit in our mouths; we*
> *want to clear our lungs.*

APPLICATION: Experiment with euphony and cacophony. Reenter one of your writings. Read it aloud. Listen to the sounds of the letters in your words. Analyze how these sounds make you feel. Slowly read several sentences aloud. Roll the sounds around in your mouth like sweet milk, like lemon juice, like an old wine. Do the sounds fit your meaning? Find synonyms for the nouns. Reread it aloud again. Speculate which words fit best. Find synonyms for the verbs. Repeat the process.

## Examples or Illustrations

EXAMPLES OR ILLUSTRATIONS are nuggets inserted into a piece of writing at just the right moment to make a point clear. Too many examples make writing monotonous; too few make it confusing. I remember once working with fifth graders. My mantra went something like this, "If your writing is flat, you can make it fat by...!" We brainstormed words for flat: *thin, superficial, plain vanilla, dull, uninteresting,* among others. Then we brainstormed ways we could fatten up a piece: by adding details, dialogue, facts, descriptions, and so forth. With that preliminary work out of the way, the kids recited the short incantation ending with a way to fatten their writing. Then they gave it a go.

All went along swimmingly until we reached "examples and illustrations." They had a terrible time understanding how to use examples or illustrations. They kept getting mixed up with details or description, even with facts. Right then, in the act of teaching, I hit upon an idea. I invited the kids to find a flat sentence in their writing and underline it. I explained that it need not be incorrect or ungrammatical, just boring. One fellow offered:

*My little brother loves me.*

Perfect. Nothing wrong with the sentence, but it lay there

on the page without zip, zing, or verve. I wrote his sentence on the board.

"How do you know he loves you?" I asked.

After much thinking and lots of body maneuvering, he said, "Well, when I come home from school and get off the bus, he comes running out of the house, hugs my legs, and reaches up to give me a high five."

Bingo!

"You just gave a great example of how a little kid might express love."

"I did?"

"Sure. But let me teach you a trick so you can remember to add those examples in your writing sometimes. Find a boring sentence and follow it with these words: *for example.*"

Under his sentence, I wrote:

> *My little brother loves me. For example, when I get off the bus after school, he comes running out of the house, hugs my legs, and reaches up to give me a high five.*

"That's a great example," I said. "Bro must have been watching and waiting for that school bus, and kids don't do that if they don't love someone."

With that illustration as a model, the class began saying *for example* after their boring sentences. Then they wrote what followed. It worked; it clicked. It added life and depth to their writing.

APPLICATION: You could do this. Warning: At first you might overdo it. Not to worry. In time that phrase becomes internalized and drops more often from the writing, but the use of example remains.

# Explanations

EXPLANATIONS are basically statements or definitions extended by elaboration. Explanation invites a five-part layering of meaning: First, *identify* a person, an event, or an action. This is usually done by writing a statement or a definition. Second, *give reasons or supporting details*. Third, *put it in a context*. Fourth, *analyze or explore it further*. Finally, *add commentary, considerations, insights, or applications*.

Let's say you are doing something expository on the medieval period. One of the topics might be the armor worn by knights. Here is a full explanation of that topic. Notice how by following the five parts of an explanation, the writing deepens.

Basic statement:

> *Knights wore armor.*

Reasons or supporting details:

> *At first their armor was made of mail, small linked iron rings, but later knights added steel plates to protect the weakest parts of the body. Even later, in the fourteenth century, full suits completely encased them. The suit moved at the joints so the knight could run, lie down, or even ride a horse in his armor.*

Putting it in a context:

> *Knights wore their armor during battles and tournaments. Besides protection, it showed the sta-*

*tus of the knight. Richer knights wore more elabo-*
*rate armor.*

Analyzing or exploring it further:

*This suit had many parts. The helmet, which was*
*lined inside, usually with fur, had a strap that could*
*be affixed under the chin. A piece of fitted metal*
*called "bevor" came up under the nose and was*
*meant to protect the lower face. Metal shoulder pads*
*covered the shoulders and upper arms while a dou-*
*blet and back plate covered the knight's front and*
*back. A mail skirt, which permitted movement, pro-*
*tected the groin. Gauntlets covered the hand and*
*wrist while three pieces of armor protected the front*
*of the leg. They were tied in place with straps at the*
*back. Knights even wore a "sabaton" that protected*
*the foot. It was made in segments and had a point-*
*ed toe. Of course, the knight carried a sword. The*
*whole outfit weighed about seventy pounds!*

Commentary:

*I knew about knights from my fairy tale books*
*and from tales of kings and queens and kingdoms. I*
*knew they served as soldiers to the king and that*
*they lived by a strict rule of conduct and honor. I*
*even knew they had to train for many years and that*
*they wore armor. But I didn't know how heavy their*
*armor was and about the many parts. Once I*
*thought I wanted to be a knight; it seemed so impor-*
*tant and adventuresome. Now, though, all I can*
*think of is how heavy and hot they must have been*
*most of the time. And those poor horses, carrying all*

*that metal and man.*

APPLICATION: Although you would not necessarily follow all five steps each time, and you could rearrange order, this process gives you a place to begin. Revising comes later.

Practice facilitates when and how to elongate a statement or definition into an explanation. See if you have a place in your writing that could be enhanced by explanation. Compare the before and after.

FACTS can be objectively verified; they are real or actual. Every time I see the word *facts* I think of the old TV police drama *Dragnet* with Sergeant Friday saying, "Just the facts, Ma'am, just the facts." Providing factual information about an event or thing or person extends your writing and promotes understanding. In the case of *Dragnet*, it helped solve the crime. Because facts are something that have actual existence, we must be careful not "to make up facts" for any reason.

Facts are everywhere. Here is an example from *Charles Dickens: The Man Who Had Great Expectations* by Diane Stanley and Peter Vennema. Read it and underline "just the facts":

> *He [Dickens] was working there on a new novel,*
> *The Mystery of Edwin Drood. All his life he had*
> *liked to write in the morning and take long walks in*

*the afternoon. But on June 8, 1870, he returned to
the chalet after lunch and worked through the afternoon. He must have known that this was the novel
he wouldn't finish, and he just wanted to write
more.*

*That evening he suffered a massive stroke, and
the following day he died, worn out, at only fifty-
eight.*

I'm sure you underlined all but the last sentence in the
first paragraph, which is an inference, and the phrase
"worn out," which is a judgment. Everything else is fact.

APPLICATION: Find the facts in your writing. Underline
them. Do you need more?

# *Humor*

HUMOR is both difficult and dangerous to write but
well worth the effort. It is difficult because you have to
intentionally craft the writing to produce comic surprise.
Juxtapositing the expected with the unexpected first frus-
trates then satisfies the reader—but in an unforeseen way.
That's hard to do.

Humor is dangerous because you might be misunder-
stood. You intend something to be funny and the reader
doesn't get it. Think of comedians or comics you enjoy. If
the pacing and timing are correct, we chuckle or laugh out
loud. If anything is off, we are almost embarrassed at the
attempt. Cultivate your writing sense of humor by study-

ing literature— the old nurse's chatter in *Romeo and Juliet*, the discussion of the life of a goldfish by the taxi driver in *The Catcher in the Rye*, cartoons from *The New Yorker*, characters such as Falstaff or Charlie Chaplin's tramp, the taxi sequence in Will Hobbs' *Changing Latitudes*, the poetry of Shel Silverstein— or by saving examples you find to model. Humor comes from the bone. Phyllis Reynolds Naylor says, "I use humor as a way of facing problems" (125).

APPLICATION: If you have a talent, a tendency to make people laugh, by all means use it. There is an old saying in rhetoric, "It is easier to write a tragedy than it is to write a comedy." Try your hand at humor. Even a touch in a serious piece can add depth.

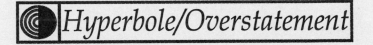

# Hyperbole/Overstatement

HYPERBOLE (OVERSTATEMENT) is a wonderful way to add wit, depth, and breadth to writing. HYPERBOLE comes from the Greek and means *to overshoot*. The best example of hyperbole is the tall tale. Everything is so exaggerated; kids and adults alike understand the concept.

My favorite tall tale, beside classics such as Pecos Bill, is *The Gullywasher* by Joyce Rossi. A grandfather, who had once been a *vaquero*, entertains his granddaughter with outrageous stories of how he got wrinkles, white hair, and best of all, his round belly. He claims he ate some hard kernels of corn followed by chile peppers. The hot chiles made the corn pop and his stomach kept getting bigger and bigger!

(Can't you just see those tinfoil corn poppers?)

We play with language this way all the time. I once told one of my curious college students that when I have my hair highlighted, I take my silky terrier along for highlights too. Writers contend that hyperbole is not so much a way of writing as a way of seeing the world; it distorts the truth by stretching it, but it also underscores it.

Jack Prelutsky advises young poets to

> *Exaggerate. This is one of the easiest techniques.*
> *You can make almost anything funny if you stretch*
> *your imagination and amplify your idea with silly*
> *and wild descriptions.* (Janeczko, 94)

APPLICATION: Find a place in your writing to exaggerate. Blow it up until it bursts. See if you have anything worth saving.

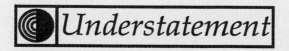

# Understatement

UNDERSTATEMENT, *meiosis* or *to make less,* the contrary to hyperbole, also comes from the Greek. As its name implies, it deliberately represents something as less important or of lesser magnitude than it really is. To understate allows the meaning to expand within the reader because the words on the page do not really mean what they say. (Hyperbole does this, too.)

Perhaps the best example of understatement in all of literature comes from Robert Frost. In "Out Out," Frost ends his narrative poem about the accidental death of a farm boy with these words:

> *Little – less – nothing! and that ended it.*
> *No more to build on there. And they, since they*
> *Were not the one dead, turned to their affairs.*

Consider all that is not said. Deconstructing these three lines, we think of the parents, their hopes and dreams for the boy, the guilt of the sister. We think how heartless are those who *turned to their affairs*, yet we identify. We realize how we go on with our lives in the face of tragedy because we must; we are human. Had Frost written all that into his poem, it would have been overly sentimental or didactic, a poor, not a great poem. As it stands, all meaning happens in the reader.

In the *Bible* we find, *Jesus wept*. What an understatement! Think about everything those two words imply. Jesus, son of God, involved in a human act that connotes weakness. Yet the reader knows Jesus is not displaying weakness but strength and compassion as he cries for Mary and for us all. We are compelled by the understatement to almost gasp at its meaning. Had the passage been written, *Jesus, Son of God, cried copiously*, the reader would not get the syntactical exclamation point.

LITOTES are a form of understatement. Kids use them without knowing they are a bona fide form of figurative language. When adolescents say "bad" meaning "great" or when they say "He's no Olympian" when they mean "he can't even catch a ball," they are stating a truth by denying its contrary. While the word comes from the Greek meaning *plain*, the device comes from the Anglo-Saxons. In *Beowulf* Hrothgar describes Grendel's ghastly dwelling by saying, "This is not a pleasant place." That's a perfect litote.

APPLICATION: Trying hyperbole and understatement will help you realize that sometimes more is not better, that occasionally depth may be achieved by writing less, by choosing words and figurative language with care. Puffing up writing when puffiness is uncalled for can produce poor writing, yet swelling a passage to aid comprehension can produce something good. Once again, it comes down to this old adage, "It's not what you do; it's the way that you do it."

# Imagery

IMAGERY means only what it is, unlike metaphor which means something other than what it is, or symbol that means what it is and something more.

• Image: The shaggy old dog rubs his back against the crooked picket fence.

• Metaphor: Some dirty old dog stole my brand new wallet.

• Symbol: You can't teach an old dog new tricks.

Imagery creates mental pictures for the reader by way of the senses. In Jerry Spinelli's award winning YA novel *Stargirl*, the "bunny hop" sequence layers image upon image to reinforce the power of Stargirl. Notice the depth of this sequence:

> ...and out came the sounds of that old teen dance standard: the bunny hop. Within seconds a long

line was snaking across the dance floor. Stargirl led the way. And suddenly it was December again, and she had the school in her spell.

....The line curled back and forth across the net-less tennis courts. Stargirl began to improvise. She flung her arms to a make-believe crowd like a celebrity on parade. She waggled her fingers at the stars. She churned her fists like an egg-beater. Every action echoed down the line behind her. The three hops of the bunny became three struts of a vaudeville vamp. Then a penguin waddle. Then a tippy-toed priss. Every new move brought new laughter from the line.

...To delighted squeals, Stargirl led them off the parquet dance floor onto the other courts — and then through the chain-link fence and off the tennis courts altogether. Red carnations and wrist cor-sages flashed as the line headed onto the practice putting green of the golf course. The line doodled around the holes, in and out of sidepools of lantern light. From the dance floor it seemed to be more than it was: one hundred couples, two hundred peo-ple, four hundred dancing legs seemed to be a single festive flowery creature, a fabulous millipede. And then there was less and less to see as the head van-ished and the rest curled through the fringe of the light and followed, like the tail of a powder-blue dragon, into the darkness. (171-172)

When you can write like that, you have arrived.

Barbara Charbula, in her book *Before the Test*, describes

how she taught fourth graders to call upon their senses when writing about cleaning their rooms. They did and had fun to boot. When these same kids went into the state-mandated test, they remembered and wrote with depth using sensory imagery. It works the same way for older writers!

APPLICATION: Foster the process by treating yourself to rich, sensory experiences. Smell wisteria, taste *crème fraiche*, run your hand over velvet, listen to birds in the morning and cars at night, gaze, peer, goggle, gape, and patently gawk at everything. Then capture those pictures with your pen. Exposing yourself to auditory, tactile, olfactory, gustatory, kinesthetic, visual, and proprioceptive stimuli in short bursts or for fun more often than not morphs into your writing.

## Irony

IRONY is a close cousin to hyperbole and litotes. Coming to us from Greek comedy, *eiron* was a character who used understatement to seem stupidly humble but who eventually triumphed over the *alazon*, the stupid braggart. Quite simply irony means its contrary. While not a device to be used by the young writer just coming to know the true meaning and extent of words in a hopefully, ever-developing vocabulary, this device is favored by the more advanced writer because it invites ambiguity and challenge, enables a manipulating of the *persona*, and all man-

ner of machinations with point of view. Irony is the ulti-
mate use of inference because you must write with an
unwritten intention and the reader must read between the
lines. Thus, it demands intelligent collaboration. Shakespeare used irony in most plays. For example, when
Othello speaks the famous line:

> *Then must you speak*
> *Of one that lov'd not wisely but too well;*
> *Of one not easily jealous....*

> ( Act V. Sc.2, Lines 343-45)

This after he killed Desdemona.

Deep, universal irony lives in the famous "Love is
blind" line spoken by Speed in *The Two Gentlemen of Verona*
(Act II, Sc. 1, Line 78). And deeper still is the irony in the
lines Romeo speaks in *Romeo and Juliet* because we know
that he is about to hear the news that Juliet is dead.

> *If I may trust the flattering truth of sleep,*
> *My dreams presage some joyful news at*
> *hand....*(Act V, Sc.1, Lines1-2)

*The Map of the World* by Jane Hamilton contains almost
unbearable irony. One mistake affects the lives of everyone
even remotely involved. As the novel opens, Alice, a woman
torn between her needs and those of her family, is watching
her friend's two small children. In the midst of looking for
her swim suit, the first irony appears. Alice looks in

> *the dresser in the hall, an unlikely place to stash a*
> *swimming suit in summer,*

and spots her map of the world, a map she had designed as
a child. This irony is inescapable — as a child she had more
control of her world than she seems to have as an adult. For

several minutes, Alice lingers over her map, thinks about it and fingers its topography. When she gets back to the children, Lizzy, her friend's youngest, is missing. Alice runs out of the house. At the clearing she spots

> *the pink seersucker bottom just beneath the surface* [of the pond] *about fifteen feet from the beach.*
>
> *When I am forced to see those ten minutes as they actually were, when I look clearly, without the scrim of half-uttered prayer and fanciful endings, I am there, tall and gangly and clumsy and slow, crying out unintelligibly, splashing through the water to Lizzy. I had nothing of a hero's elegance or pace. As I moved I was thinking, She's fine! She's fine! She's probably looking for minnows or stones or snails so far from the shore.*

But Lizzy is not fine. Lizzy has drowned.

The power of irony as a writing device is that so often in life things are ironic: the tragic irony of the people who escaped the twin towers disaster in September only to be killed in the plane explosion a month later; the athlete who wins the race but drops of a heart attack; the woman who sells all the baby clothes only to discover she is again pregnant; the kid who just gets his driver license and has an accident.

APPLICATION: By noticing the irony around you, you can create depth by injecting it into your writing. Often things are not as they seem or expectations don't always turn out as planned. There is no simple way to regard events. Take a risk. Add some irony to your writing.

# 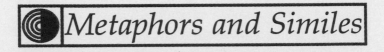Metaphors and Similes

METAPHORS and SIMILES are all about likenesses. The mind operates that way. We see one thing and it reminds us of another. We explain something, get a blank look, and immediately grab for a comparison. Both *metaphor* and *simile* set out a comparison. Metaphor implicitly makes the linkage whereas simile explicitly creates it using words such as *like* or *as*. Janet Fitch, master of likenesses, once said when interviewed by Oprah that metaphors and similes must be fresh. To paraphrase, she said if you ever heard the comparison before, to use it would be cliché. Here are several examples from her novel *White Oleander*, some explicit, some implicit, none cliché:

> *The Santa Anas blew in hot from the desert, shriveling the last of the spring grass into whiskers of pale straw.* (3)

> *Barry. When he appeared, he was so small. Smaller than a comma, insignificant as a cough.* (4)

> *As always when she read, my mother wore white, and her hair was the color of new snow against her lightly tanned skin. She stood in the shade of a massive fig tree, its leaves like hands.* (4)

> *The sun was hot through the screens when I woke up, illuminating the milky stagnant air wrapped like a towel around the morning.* (21)

> *Sergei's heart. That empty corridor, that unaired*

*room.* (319)

*I started to cut a mermaid with long, art nouveau hair from the cover of an old <u>Scientific American.</u>* (318)

*On the anvil of August, the city lay paralyzed, stunned into stupidity by the heat. The sidewalks shrank under the sun. It was a landscape of total surrender.* (361)

And this, my personal favorite, showcases her skill. To see pigeons in flight moving so systematically that she likens them to the visual signaling of flags, rings as pure mastery:

*A flight of pigeons raced across the rich carved surface of the sky, their wings beating white and gray in unison, like a semaphore. I wondered if they knew where they were going when they flew like that.* (356)

APPLICATION: Cull your writing for the tired expression. Underline it and work to transform it; give it new life through a fresh metaphor or a stunning simile.

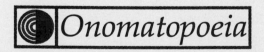

# Onomatopoeia

ONOMATOPOEIA, sometimes called ECHOISM, has two applications, one narrow and one broad. The narrow and more common understanding of *onomatopoeia* is a word that sounds like its meaning. *Buzz, hiss, lullaby* fit into this category. But in writing for depth, the broader meaning of the term rules. Here the correspondence extends to passages and longer pieces where form supports the meaning.

In writing about violence, for example, you wouldn't find a preponderance of words with liquid *L* or *R* sounds. Conversely, in a violent piece such as *The .38* by Ted Joans (Carroll & Wilson, 102-103) the sentences are short, staccato, emulating the rapid fire of a gun. Words with hard sounds, nasals, plosives, gutterals, and sibilants strike the ear like shots: *scream, glasses, outside, banging, drag, groan, beat, cuts, singe.* Likewise the anaphora, every line begins with *I hear,* raises tension and matches the rapidity of action. Thus, the entire poem takes us through the experience by exploiting sounds that correspond to the action.

Think of your favorite nursery rhyme and you'll have an example of narrow and broad onomatopoeia. *Humpty Dumpty* sounds big and awkward. We are not surprised when he falls. *Baa, baa, black sheep* uses the sound the sheep make, and Jack who is *nimble* and *quick* can indeed *jump over the candelstick.* The word *nimble* sounds like what it means as does the word *quick.*

> *Hickory, dickory dock,*
> *The mouse ran up the clock.*
> *The clock struck one,*
> *The mouse ran down,*
> *Hickory, dictory dock.*

*Hickory* exemplifies broad onomatopoeia because its rhythm approximates that of a metronome. Without using the word *ticking,* the reader hears it in the rhythm. The poem begins and ends with the same line, much like a clock beginning at twelve and ending at twelve. It is a circular poem that resembles the circular face of a clock. The striking of *one* is somewhat jarring, especially because of the muscular blend *str.* (Words such as *strain, strength, strangle, strike, strive* are powerful words that often sound like what they mean.) Just that single sound *one*, just that single-syllable word, works. Eleven strikes or seven strikes loses the drama.

In *Prodigal Summer*, Barbara Kingsolver treats readers to onomatopoeia so intricately bound to the story, we almost miss its power. Even the character's name *Lusa* sounds deep and full of meaning, carrying with it that liquid *L* sound.

> *Lusa stood on the front porch, watching rain pour over the front eave in long silver strings. The gabled roof of the farmhouse – her farmhouse – was made of grooved tin that shunted the water into channels running down its steep sides. Some of the trickles poured over as clear filaments, like fishing line, while others looked beaded, like strings of pearls. She'd put buckets on the wide steps under some of the trickles and discovered that each string of droplets tapped out its own distinctive rhythm in its bucket. All morning, the rhythm of each stream never changed – it only grew softer as the bucket filled, then returned to its hollow rat-tat-a-rat-tat-tat! After she emptied the bucket.* (101)

APPLICATION: Enter your writing. Try your hand at narrow and broad onomatopoeia. Use Kingsolver, Joans, or Mother Goose as your models.

# 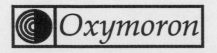 *Oxymoron*

OXYMORON comes from the Greek meaning *pointedly foolish*. More specifically *oxus* means *sharp* and *moros* means *dull*. This figure of speech combines contradictory or incongruous words: *jumbo shrimp, freezer burn*, or even *drag race, almost perfect, easy problem*.

How can antithetical words create depth? Just this way: Two contradictory terms — adjective against noun as in *urban cowboy* — allow you "to go further, not to a comparison but to an antithesis, forcing the mind to run the gamut of an axis of meaning in seeking some vehemence of expression" (Hughes, 34).

Hughes, in his book *More on Oxymoron*, borrows an oxymoron from Goethe,

> *Architecture is frozen music,*

and goes on to elaborate it. In doing so, he forces his mind, and ours, to run the gamut:

> *Water is temporarily frozen, often in tremendous natural patterns and shapes, revealing mathematical structures, whereas music runs like water, never repeating itself exactly. Ice is quiet and is often perceived in, say, the silence of winter in the woods. Goethe's antithesis of frost and organized sound illuminates the permanent and decorative art of building. It is a magical idea that overnight a frost could still and silence music into monochro-*

*matic architecture* (36).

Expand several oxymora (Hughes's book offers many)—perhaps Robert Southey's

> *They agreed to differ.*

Others you might try:

- This is about as useful as a plastic frying pan.
- That went over like a lead balloon.
- Some people do things accidentally on purpose.
- *Men's evil manners live in brass; their virtues we write in water.* (Shakespeare)
- *Music: cathedrals in sound.* (Alfred Brumeau)
- *I've got a good memory for forgetting.* (Robert Louis Stevenson)
- *All this relaxation has exhausted me.* (Ashleigh Brilliant)
- *Punctuality is the thief of time.* (Oscar Wilde)

APPLICATION: To write an oxymoron takes practice. If you incorporate this figure of speech into your writing, you will achieve a higher level of sophistication and elaboration.

# Personification

PERSONIFICATION, the attributing of life to lifeless or non-human things, is the easiest figure of speech to learn. Toddlers often admonish a toy as if it were alive. The term *personification*, from the Greek *prosopopeia*, means that abstract concepts or inanimate objects may be spoken to or written about as if endowed with human qualities. It is easy to remember; just think of "person" in the word *personification*.

Adding personification to writing is an ancient art. Primitive peoples told stories about the sun, moon, stars in order to explain the phenomena they saw around them. Susanne Langer attributes this to the symbolizing mind, an essential act (41). Why can't the moon be sentient and cause the oceans to ebb and flow? Why can't *the wind tiptoe between poplars* as James Wright suggests? Why can't *you hear the silverware catching its eager breath inside the sleeping drawer*, as William Matthews contends? Why can't *the old snow get up and move taking its birds with it*, as W. S. Merwin writes? (Nims, 60). The freshness of thought is so much better than the more mundane: The wind blew between the trees, the silverware is in the drawer, the snow melted and the birds flew away. When appropriately used, personification improves your writing.

Once, when teaching a model lesson on personification to third graders, I invited them to fold a paper in half and make a list of things on one side. They wrote, predictably, what they saw around them: *desk, pencil, window, bulletin board*. When I asked them to add things from outside, they wrote: *grass, wind, sidewalk, school bus*. Then they opened their paper and listed next to each "thing" something a person might do. So desks walked, pencils screamed, windows cried, bulletin boards blabbed, the grass shouted "ouch" when someone stepped on it, the wind worried, the sidewalk adopted a crack, and the school bus lied. By the time we shared, the kids were clear on the concept. This exercise works for all writers when they need a fresh look.

APPLICATION: Take the nouns from a paragraph in one of your writings and list them down one side of a folded paper. Open the paper and write a list of things a person would do. Analyze how the match *freshens* your writing.

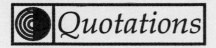

QUOTATIONS FROM OTHER SOURCES are necessary in some modes of writing and including them should become second nature. Quoting adds credibility to a composition if the quotation is accurate and apt. Three important things to remember about using quotations:

• Introduce the quotation;
• Cite the quotation accurately;
• Explain the connection between the quotation and whatever you are saying in your writing. For excellent ideas on how to teach quotations and proverbs to young writers, read Charbula's *Before the Test*, especially pages 26-31.

APPLICATION: Keep a notebook of quotations: "Top Ten Quotes Notes." When you come across something memorable, something you like, copy it. Periodically take the headlines from the newspaper and fit a quote to the headline. Be sure clear on the connection. Do this often. Try it with your writing, and you will begin to see how quotations boost your meaning.

#  Repetition

REPETITION is the drum of remembering. It has to do with the heart beat. Think of the way children repeat: *bye-bye* as if the second *bye* confirms the act of leaving; *ma ma*, the second *ma* for emphasis; *cheep, cheep* to imitate a sound. Notice the use of repetition in this traditional verse used to entertain children for decades as parents cleaned toes or relatives and friends played with the babies:

> *This little piggy went to market;*
> *This little piggy stayed home.*
> *This little piggy had roast beef;*
> *This little piggy had none.*
> *And, this little piggy went, "Wee, wee, wee!"*
> *All the way home!*

First comes the repetitive phrase followed by the verb and then we hear the difference. Without that difference, unvarying repetition would be monotonous and unpalatable. Good repetition has a sameness and a difference. Note the almost inborn tendency for eurhythmics. We move our the body to the harmony of lines. Finally, don't miss the use of the high frequency vowel sound in *wee*. Hence the child delights and the child remembers.

So, too, with repetition in writing. It emphasizes, it shows a dwelling upon something, it makes us stop and listen; we identify and we remember. Effective repetition repeats a word, a phrase, even a sentence for rhetorical emphasis:

> *"I don't hate it," Quentin said quickly, at once, immediately; "I don't hate it," he said. I don't hate it, he thought, panting in the cold air, the iron New England dark; I don't I don't; I don't hate it! I don't hate it!* (378).

In the above, the final paragraph in William Faulkner's *Absolom, Absolom!*, Shreve asks, "Why do you hate the South?" and Quentin gives his obsessive reply. Faulkner uses repetition to get into the mind of Quentin, showing his determination to convince himself that he does not hate the South. This is effective use of repetition.

Ineffective repetition happens when writers repeat themselves as if they have forgotten what they wrote, or as if they think the reader did not get the meaning the first time or the second time. Repeating in this way insults or bores the reader and is not considered good writing.

APPLICATION: Reread you writing. Use a green marker to signal effective repetition; use a red maker to highlight something you have said before or something you have said in the same way. Revise accordingly.

## Sentences

SENTENCES. A sentence is the shape words take when they are bunched together, and we bunch them in certain ways in English. To know what a sentence *is* is the work of the academician; to know what a sentence *does* is the work of a writer. You need to make sentences do what you want them to do; you need to control them and organize them for your purpose.

If sentences represent an act of the mind and we have over 100,000,000,000 neurons in that mind/brain, then we know expressing our meaning can happen in billions of ways. That is exciting.

In a small but powerful book written by Alan C. Purves in the seventies called *How Porcupines Make Love: Notes on a Response-Centered Curriculum*, Purves talks about how different people make different judgments about things. He goes on to say, "Scientific research shows that there are a minimum of 500,000,000,000 possible different responses to a given text. That's at least 200 different responses for everybody in the world!" (42) A sentence is a response to someone, some thing, some thought, something read, and those figures fit the possibilities of the sentences you write. Therefore, the expressiveness of a sentence can emphasize or de-emphasize your meaning.

There are long sentences and short sentences and everything in-between. Long sentences convey drama, deep thought by embedding related thoughts into, before, or after the kernel, or they convey tireless energy. Short sentences strike us as choppy, sometimes childlike, or as bursts of meaning or energy.

Also when thinking about sentences, consider the use of connectives. The way sentences, like kids, hang together make a statement. If writers have no other transition than *and* in their repertoire, their sentences might be humdrum or may strike the ear as babyish, primitive even. Yet the connective *and*, the great grammatical unifier, can be impressive, as in the first chapter of Genesis:

> *In the beginning God created the heaven and the earth. And the earth was without form, and void; and darkness was upon the face of the deep. And the Spirit of God moved upon the face of the waters. And God said, "Let there be light": and there was light.*

Conclusion: it is not what you do; it's the way you do it.

Fool around with sentence structure. Invert normal word order to turn things around in the mind of the reader. "I have learned that there is always something new to try with my writing. I think that's part of the kick of writing—trying something new and seeing what happens when we do" (Janeczko, 1). Milton did.

> *Him the Almighty Power*
> *Hurled headlong flaming from the ethereal sky*

This word order sounds awkward, even ugly, but Milton was writing of Satan and wanted the words and their inverted order to convey the evil of Satan.

Parentheticals, which can be punctuated by parentheses, dashes, or commas, interrupt normal syntax—word order. When that happens, the aside gets noticed. E. L. Konigsburg achieves this effect in her Newbery winner *The View from Saturday*. In the first chaper, Mrs. Eva Marie Olinski explains how she chose her team for the sixth-grade Academic Bowl:

> ...*To the district superintendent of schools, she gave a bad answer, but she did that only once, only to him, and if that answer was not good, her reason for giving it was* (1).

Konigsburg off sets parenthetical information with commas to show the complexity of Olinski's thinking.

> *...This was the last Saturday in May, and some robot — human or electronic — had checked the calendar instead of the weather report and had turned on the air-conditioning* (2).

The em dash humorously indicates the stupidity of turning on the A/C by calendar not temperature.

> *...She watched with baited (and visible) breath as the commissioner placed his hand into the large clear glass bowl. His college class ring knocked bottom. (Had the room been two degrees colder, the glass would have shattered it.)* (3)

Parentheses show digressions, asides, that call attention to the frigid room.

APPLICATION: Go to something you are writing. Replace commas with dashes, dashes with parenthesis, parenthesis with commas. Mix and match with abandon. Reread and consider if or how the marks change things.

You also need to think about how sentences link to each other. (See Chapter Four on coherence.)

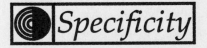

# Specificity

SPECIFICITY makes plain the writer's ability to control details. Writing broad, general, or abstract statements often confuses or loses readers, whereas writing specifics ensures comprehension. Karl Taylor advises a movement from *flu-*

*ency* to *specificity* to *organization*. So heed that advice. Get writing, get comfortable with writing, and then add the specifics: Name your uncle, tell the exact location of the accident, share the color of the eyes, and the gesture that indicates helplessness. Writing is not so much saying memorable things as saying things in memorable ways. Then, after the pages are full, organize them.

In writing this book, I wrote, wrote, wrote. Then I added specifics from writers and examples from literature. After deciding on a way to organize it—chapters and alphabetical arrangement—I began doing research to support what I had written. On the last revision, I worked with the words, wanting them to say exactly what I meant. (I found some snafus!) As Don Graves, award winning nonfiction writer, often says, "The problem is not with writing, the problem with writing is NOT writing." Writing often yields fluency, which in time, with practice and good instruction and good intention, evolves into specificity, organization, often supported by research. Julia Cameron reminds us, "Specificity is like breathing: one breath at a time, that is how life is built" (52). I might add, and that is how writing is built.

APPLICATION: Try building a paragraph or two in your writing. Everywhere you can, add the specific—name the name; don't use *white*, write *eggshell*; don't use *called*, write *hailed*; don't use *girl*, write *Emma Sue*; don't use, *We went down the road*, write *We bumped along Farm-to-Market 287*.

# Statistics

STATISTICS are facts expressed in numbers. Quantitative data are powerful proofs. Even little children can collect data. They create alphabetical graphs of their first names. For example, a child writes his/her first name on a card. Along the wall are alphabet cards in alphabetical order. The child looks at the first letter in his or her name and tapes the name card under the correct letter of the alphabet. My card would go under *J*; my husband's would go under *E*. Then the class counts and records the number of names under each letter. When they finish, they have statistics about the first names in their class.

Sometimes people think statistics are boring. They may be, but they don't have to be. Erik Bruun proves that in his book *Texas*.

> *Amarillo is a quirky place. Local businessmen commissioned artists in 1974 to bury 10 Cadillacs in a wheat field along Route 66, with their back ends popping up from the ground at a 52-degree angle (the same angle as the Great Pyramid in Egypt). The businessmen called it a salute to the American automobile, and "Cadillac Ranch" has become one of Texas's best-known attractions.*

APPLICATION: For that touch of veracity, think about adding statistics to your writing.

# Symbol

Symbolic images are usually concrete objects that stand for abstractions. For example, a rock may symbolize strength. The most archetypal symbols are natural ones such as fire, water, wind, and the earth itself. When used in a story or composition, the reader's mind kicks into another level of meaning. Writers working with symbols admit they diversify their thinking—a welcome characteristic for a writer.

There are three types of symbols:

• NONCE SYMBOLS are used for the moment; their meaning is determined by context. In a story I am writing, I use *pickle* as a nonce symbol representing individuality. It works in context because the character always eats a pickle, not candy or ice cream like the other kids, when she comes to the local hangout. In any other context *pickle* would not necessarily represent individuality.

• PERSONAL SYMBOLS, chosen by writers, are used again and again. William Faulkner likens the locomotive to change and honeysuckle to the sensuous; Linda Pastan weaves leaves and bread into her poems to represent home, the passing of time, patience, resurrection.

• CHANGING SYMBOLS are those that stand for something during one period of time but something else in another period of time. The letter V is a good example. V, especially making a V by separating your index and middle fingers, stood for victory in the forties but a mere twenty years later that same sign meant peace.

APPLICATION: Find the recurring symbols of your favorite authors. Analyze their effectiveness. Develop a sense of symbol for your writing by thinking of something meaningful to you and using it to represent something in your writing.

SYNESTHESIA uses one sense to tell about another. We think early peoples were less likely to compartmentalize sensual experiences than contemporary people. We smell, we taste, we hear, whereas they welcomed the overlapping of sense perceptions the way children do.

My favorite example of children using synesthesia comes from an article in *Learning* called "Linda's Rewrite" by Charles Suhor. Linda, a third grade student suffering through many drafts about spring, writes in her third revision,

> *"Spring is here. I like it. Flowers are all over.*
> *Flowers feel like rain."*

That last sentence is stunning, a perfect example of synesthesia, but unfortunately the teacher nixes it. So in revision four, Linda draws a person touching a flower. But Suhor tells us that for the teacher "pictures don't count."

Susanne Langer suggests that there is a tendency for children "to read a vague sort of meaning into pure visual and auditory forms." Remembering her earliest recollections of chairs and tables as having looks and moods such as "a stern armchair," she explains:

> *Childhood is the great period of synesthesia; sounds and colors and temperatures, forms and feelings, may have certain characters in common, by which a vowel may "be" of a certain color, a tone may "be" large or small, low or high, bright or dark, etc. There is a strong tendency to form associations among sensa that are not practically fixed in the world, even to confuse such random impressions* (123).

When you use synesthesia, you add a touch of originality to your work. You also startle the reader into another level of knowing. As you might expect, we find synesthesia most among poets and children. May Swenson describes daffodils as

> *yellow telephones...ringing shrill with light*

and T. S. Eliot gives us something to think about when he writes of a street lamp that

> *beats like a fatalistic drum.*

When I read these lines, I realized how the poets and I coacted. They created the synesthesia, I co-created the image. I could see daffodils as old-time upright telephones, and I could feel Eliot's pulsing light. I get the same feeling when children laugh at Judi Barrett's book title *Cloudy with a Chance of Meatballs* or when I see a Klee painting, especially his gestural painting *Secret Letters*. Best book about a character not understanding synesthesia (and I rarely give negative examples) is *Emily's Art* by Peter Catalonotto.

Why can't a dog have rabbit ears?

Sometimes we use synesthesia without realizing it. For instance, when we talk about a "sweet smile" or a "sour expression," we are using synesthesia because we are quite literally "sensing together."

Poet Maxine Kumin writes of her father as

*a man who wore hard colors recklessly.*

Color is not hard or soft — we see color not feel it. Or do we?

APPLICATION: Move from the predictable: hearing music, touching books, seeing clouds, tasting apples, and smelling roses. Try touching music, hearing clouds, tasting roses. Go through a section of your work, dig up images, and replant them by scrambling sensa. See what happens.

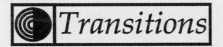

# Transitions

TRANSITIONS are important not only for carrying the depth of writing but also for carrying its logic. Typically writers think of transitions as words such as *first, next, then, finally,* but we need to move further along to more sophisticated transitional phrases and transitional paragraphs. Writing something such as *Thinking ahead, I moved on to...* rather than *Next...* certainly conveys a deeper, more cosmopolitan voice. Likewise, functional paragraphs act as chunks of transitional information, so readers are able to follow the logic of the composition. In a real sense, transitional phrases and paragraphs take the reader's mind by the hand to lead it into meaningful knowing.

Transitions may be made by
  • Connecting ideas;
  • Repeating or rephrasing key words or terms;
  • Using parallel structure;
  • Employing introductory phrases or clauses.
Here are frequently used transitions for handy reference:

  • to show something additional: *and, also, besides, further, in addition, next, too, first, second;*

  • to prepare for an example: *for example, for instance, to illustrate, specifically, in fact, in turn;*

  • to compare or contrast: *also, in the same way, similarly, likewise , but, however, on the other hand, even though, on the contrary, yet;*

  • to summarize: *in short, to summarize, in summary, in conclusion, to sum up, therefore;*

  • to indicate time: *after, as, before, during, later, finally, meanwhile, then, while, immediately,* and sequence words;

  • to give a place or a direction: *about, above, close, over, nearby, to the right, beyond;*

  • to show a relationship: *so, therefore, if, thus, as a result.*

APPLICATION: While you need transitional words in your writing, try to sophisticate them by finding the words listed above and trying your hand at turning them into longer phrases or clauses.

#  Word Choice

WORD CHOICE is the writer's major asset. Think of your work as marble, think of yourself as a sculptor, and think of the act of writing as letting the right words out. Michelangelo said, "I saw the angel in the marble and I just chiseled till I set him free."

With over a billion English words—experts tell us we use about 200,000 of them regularly—we have a pretty good chance of saying what we mean. For you, though, it is not so much saying something with words as *making* something out of words. That's why a piece of writing is called a composition; it is not unlike an artist considering design, layout, and color for a painting, or a musician considering notes, harmony, or beat when composing a song. An artist uses a canvas, paint or some such medium, and a sense of organization to *make* the painting work. The musician does the same with notes and chords. You *make your meaning* with the right words. The vitality of the writer's vocabulary either leaves the writing dead on the page or alive with meaning.

And words have levels. Ken Macrorie calls this *elevated* or *kitchen* language. Determine formal or colloquial words by intent and audience not by length of word or level of difficulty. The biggest word is not always the best, but a well placed, precise word is a sweet note. You should work in tandem with the dictionary and thesaurus, but above all, you should own the words you use.

Sometimes ideas come from authors. They snuggle the idea into the text of a novel from time to time. In Amy Tan's *The Bonesetter's Daughter*, she records a conversation between Art, who has a doctorate in linguistics, and Ruth.

> [Art says]"... *I've always loved words, the power of them.*"
>
> "*So what's your favorite word?*"
>
> "*Hm, that's an excellent question.*" *He fell quiet, stroking his beard in thought.*
>
> *Ruth was thrilled. He was probably groping for a word that was arcane and multisyllabic, one of those crossword items that could be confirmed only in the Oxford English Dictionary.*
>
> "*Vapors,*" *he said at last.*
>
> "*Vapors?*" *Ruth thought of chills and cold, mists and suicide ghosts. That was not a word she would have chosen.*
>
> "*It appeals to all the senses,*" *he explained.* "*It can be opaque but never solid. You can feel it, but it has no permanent shape. It might be hot or cold. Some vapors smell terrible, others quite wonderful. Some are dangerous, others are harmless. Some are brighter than others when burned, mercury versus sodium, for instance. Vapors can go up your nose with a sniff and permeate your lungs. And the sound of the word, how it forms on your lips, teeth, and tongue vaporzzzzzz — it lilts up, then lingers and fades. It's perfectly matched to its meanings.*"
>
> "*It is,*" *Ruth agreed.* "*Vaporzzzz,*" *she echoed,*

*savoring the buzz on her tongue.* (26-27)

When I read that conversation, which continues on for several more paragraphs becoming both scientific and philosophical with Ruth ultimately offering *onomatopoeia* as her favorite word because she once spelled it correctly in a spelling bee, I marked it for three reasons. It exemplifies onomatopoeia beautifully; it exemplifies how a word can expand meaning, in this case characterization. Then it occurred to me that Tan gave writers a wonderful idea— that is, choose your favorite word and go on to justify your choice.

APPLICATION: Why not write down your favorite word? Use Tan's excerpt as an example to elaborate the word. If nothing else this exercise raises consciousness about words and their power. (I'd choose *juxtapose*.)

# Chapter 3
## Show Don't Tell

There's an old adage in writing: "Don't tell, but show." ... Writing is not psychology. We do not talk "about" feelings. Instead the writer feels and through her words awakens those feelings in the reader. The writer takes the reader's hand and guides him through the valley of sorrow and joy without ever having to mention those words.

—Natalie Goldberg,
poet and writing teacher

# *Show Don't Tell*

SHOW DON'T TELL, also called "the dramatic method," is perhaps one of the oldest pieces of advice offered by master writers to rookies.

Truth is, the old "show don't tell" adage lives as the original virtual reality long before *Star Trek* or *Star Wars* and makes sense if considered that way. Think about it. Our brains receive and process sensory signals from our environment through our five senses in order to make sense of our world, our experiences. Good writing that shows, takes us through the experience; it excites the brain by wrapping pictures and sounds, tastes, smells and movements around us and immersing our senses so the writing actually creates another world. Catherine Drinker Bowen, biographer and writer on musical subjects, puts it more poetically,

> *Writing is not apart from living. Writing is kind of double living.*

Phrased in the positive, this showing, this going through the experience, causes us to feel an immediacy, a vitality, an authenticity. When we're finished reading writing that shows, we think, "I wish this wouldn't end." Flip-flopping to the negative, writing devoid of this showing seems plastic and bores the brain. If we even finish it (and most often we don't) we find ourselves yawning and asking, "What did I just read?"

APPLICATION: But there's an irony in "show don't tell."

The maxim itself tells. It's right up there with "develop your writing" and "liven those verbs." There is no doubt about it—the advice is sound—it's just too abstract. Therein lies the rub. What can we do to show not tell? Following are five ways to practice this showing:

- Analyze the work of published authors;
- Compare telling writing to showing writing;
- Recognize and use "show don't tell" as an elaboration technique;
- Identify telling parts in your writing;
- Replace the telling parts of your writing with showing parts.

## Analyzing the Work of Published Authors

When examining the work of published authors, start with Mark Twain's words,

> *Don't say the old lady screamed. Bring her on and let her scream.*

It's a great quote that begs great questions, "What does Twain mean?" "How might we describe her?" "Where is she?" "What words could we use to hear her scream?" "Why is she screaming?" It's a fun exercise to try both ways—tell about the old lady, then bring her on and show her off.

Will Hobbs, noted YA author, says it this way,

> *Let's say I almost drowned last summer, when a rip tide was taking me out to sea, and I'm trying to*

> *tell a reader what it was like: "I was drowning. It*
> *was really bad. I thought I was going to die..."*
> *Now, is my writing coming to life? Does the reader*
> *feel what is was like? Not really. Did I tell, or did I*
> *show? I told. I didn't use the five senses. Where's*
> *the taste of salt water, the powerful tug of that rip*
> *tide, the voices at the shore dimming, the squawk of*
> *a gull?* (Hobbs, 19)

What Hobbs suggests is pure virtual reality. No one really wants to experience drowning, but if the writer crafts the experience by showing not telling, then we experience the virtual reality of drowning. It works this way because of the sensory signals the words conjure; the brain makes a connection and consequently makes meaning. Since our senses are the primary information gatherers constantly sending signals to the brain, Hobbs invites us to stimulate all five senses through the power of words. That way, after the brain has reconstructed and synthesized the signals, it identifies and we understand. Helping that connection equals good writing.

Once you awaken to "show don't tell" in your writing, it becomes an excellent technique for literary analysis. Imagine quibbling over colonist Edward Winslow's letter to a friend in England, pointing out how much more powerful it would have been had he taken his friend through the experience of the "harvest being gotten in" instead of just telling him. Or picture a group of writers eagerly identifying examples of showing not telling in *The Red Badge of Courage*. After reading,

> *One of the wounded men had a shoeful of blood. He*

> *hopped like a schoolboy in a game. He was laughing*
> *hysterically....* (Crane 44)

it is unlikely you would settle for,

> *One man was shot in the foot. He was in pain.*

APPLICATION: Go through your writing. To show not tell, employ the strategy *Prove Its!* (See page 2.) Put the lady on the stage and let her scream.

## Compare Telling Writing with Showing Writing

One of the attributes of showing writing is specificity and concern for detail. Using comparisons of different versions of the same story makes this plain. For example, choose a passage that describes a character from a fairy tale or folk tale, one with many versions, such as *Cinderella* or *Little Red Riding Hood*. I choose *Baba Yaga*:

Version One:

> *When they had entered the hut the old witch threw*
> *herself down on the stove, stretched out her bony*
> *legs and said....* (Sierra, 97)

Version Two:

> *When Vasilisa entered the hut, Baba Yaga was*
> *already sitting in her chair by the fire. Her black*
> *eyes sparkled as she fixed them on the girl.* (Mayer)

Version Three:

> *Suddenly the forest was filled with a terrible noise,*
> *and Baba Yaga came flying through the trees. She*
> *was riding in a great iron mortar and driving it*

> with a pestle, and as she rode, she swept away her
> trail with a kitchen broom. (Winthrop, 17)

Finally we come to Version Four. This version is embedded in the penetrating psychological study *Women Who Run With the Wolves: Myths and Stories of the Wild Woman Archetype* by Clarissa Pinkola Estes.

> Now the Baba Yaga was a very fearsome
> creature. She traveled not in a chariot, not in a
> coach, but in a cauldron shaped like a mortar which
> flew along all by itself. She rowed this vehicle with
> an oar shaped like a pestle, and all the while she
> swept out the  tracks of where she'd been with a
> broom made of long-dead persons' hair.
>
> And the cauldron flew through the sky with
> Baba Yaga's own greasy hair flying behind. Her
> long chin curved up and her long nose curved
> down, and they met in the middle. She had a tiny
> white goatee and warts on her skin from her trade
> in toads. Her brown-stained fingernails were thick
> and ridged like roofs, and so curled over she could
> not make a fist. (77)

While the first three versions, taken from children's literature, rely on pictures to convey most of the detail, even the youngest writer will see how ably Estes crafted her Baba Yaga. From that opening, somewhat telling statement, through the layers of detail that prove Baba Yaga's fearsomeness, Estes shows.

APPLICATION: After an exercise such as this, you will rarely write, "She was a witch." Your journey into the lushness of writing and literature is enriched. Reenter your writing to show not tell. Talk your readers through the experience. Let the reader fear your Baba Yaga.

## Recognize and Use "Show Don't Tell" as an Elaboration Technique

I opened the novel in full view of the writing class. "Take out some paper and write down these sentences," I invited.

> *I remember the day Claire Louise started first grade....She had on a red dress....Mother made all our clothes....She had a book satchel my grandmother bought for her....That was a Saturday.* (Arnold, 7-8)

"What do you think about that writing?" I asked.

Students, who typically want to please the professor, began by tentatively, and without much enthusiasm, saying, "It's OK." But then they quickly pulled the turn-about and asked, "Whose Claire Louise?" "Why are you reading this?"

I continued to probe. "She's a character in this novel, but I really want to know what you think of the writing."

Eventually a brave soul admitted, "It sounds dull." Another agreed. Soon they determined collectively it was definitely telling not showing.

At this point I wrote the word *elaboration* on the board. I explained how showing helps the writer achieve an elaborated piece, one that reveals depth of thought. Under elaboration I wrote D.I.D. I told the students that although there are many ways to achieve this depth, these letters stood as a mnemonic device to remember at least three of them.

Their first response was *dialogue* which we had worked on previously. We talked about that, but I wanted them to explore further. After some nudges and discussion, they came up with *description, illustration,* and *detail.*

"Now I'll read the passage from the novel exactly as it was written. Listen for description, illustration, and detail."

<u>*I remember the day Claire Louise started first grade.*</u> *Everyone claims I'd have been too young to remember that, that at two years old I couldn't possibly remember Claire Louise starting school. But I do remember.* <u>*She had on a red dress.*</u> *Red was always my favorite color, still is for that matter. The dress was red checks and had a starched white collar and puffy white sleeves with white cuffs on them. And the belt that went with the dress my mother bought from the store to go with it, the dress she made herself.* <u>*Mother made all our clothes.*</u> *Mostly she made Claire Lousie's clothes and I wore them four years later. And Claire Louise even had red socks to go with her dress, and she wore her black and white saddle oxfords that my mother bought to be her school shoes.* <u>*She had a book satchel my grandmother bought for her,*</u> *and all the school supplies the drugstore had printed on the first-grade list on the lowest shelf. She had those in the book bag. She had carefully printed her name on everything that went in her bag. We watched her do*

*it, my mother and me. I sat in my mother's lap and watched Claire Louise get ready for her first day at school. <u>That was a Saturday,</u> I'm sure, because I can remember the sound of the lawn mower as Claire Louise carefully wrote her name, and my father only mowed on Saturday morning.* (Arnold, 7-8)

The students caught the big picture, the description of the narrator on her mother's lap. They reveled in all the details of color and collar, belt and satchel. They realized the mowing proved to be an illustration, a proof. Although none saw the real Claire Louise, they did see the virtual Claire Louise. (This technique can be applied to any rich piece of writing.)

APPLICATION: Take a memory and add description, illustration, and detail so that it becomes a virtual reality for the reader.

# Identify Telling Parts in Your Own Writing

Armed now with concrete examples of telling and showing, you will be better able to assess your writing. The initial act of reentry will be one of challenge. Finding examples of telling should be cause for celebration. After all, you are looking at your writing with new eyes to find parts to improve — an awesome cognitive task.

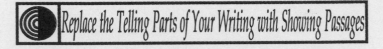

## Replace the Telling Parts of Your Writing with Showing Passages

Following is an example from Adrian's writing. He highlighted his first three sentences:

*I stayed over at Robert's house last Friday. We were going camping. That was our favorite thing to do even though we only pretended.*

On his next draft he replaced those telling parts with this showing passage:

*I was spending Friday night at Robert's house, so our camping gear was strewn across the backyard. We pretended we had pitched camp in the outback of Australia, so we called each other "mate" a lot.*

*"Ay, mate," I'd call even though we were pretty close to each other in that backyard. "Let's take a walkabout." (I had seen a movie about that.)*

*"Ay, mate," he'd call back louder. "Let's throw some shrimp on the barbee." (I saw that commercial on T.V.)*

*Finally, we went to bed. Robert had asthma and was lying in the tent on his cot wheezing like a water pump gone dry. My buddy did many things better than me, but I envied his asthmatic wheeze the most. That night he wheezed out a little tune in his sleep and I accompanied him on the drums by playing my stomach and cot.*

While Adrian did some throat clearing at first, the passage about Robert's asthma takes us through what Adrian went through. It shows voice, promise, and a grasp of the "show don't tell" concept.

The pith of the showing/telling dichotomy comes when you become facile enough to enliven your writing with powerful passages that show not tell. Writing by showing comes down to this, best said by C. S. Lewis,

> *Don't say it was delightful; make us say delightful when we've read the description. You see, all those words (horrifying, wonderful, hideous, exquisite) are only like saying to your readers, "Please will you do my job for me."* (Brodie, 64)

APPLICATION: As you reread your work, simply highlight the telling statements, decide which are fine as they are (some telling is inevitable in any piece of writing), and revise accordingly.

# Chapter 4
## Gluing it Together: Coherence

*Among the special conventions of text in any language is a wide variety of devices whose purpose is cohesion. These provide ways in which sentences may be knitted together.*

—Frank Smith,
*Writing and the Writer*

#  Coherence

COHERENCE is the Velcro® of writing. Without coherence, neither sentences nor paragraphs would make sense. Thought would be a random thing with little or no connection to any other thought. To make this concept concrete, since e-mail sometimes programs us to be less coherent — imagine two coherent sentences — one on one sentence strip, the other on another sentence strip. Mentally, adhere Velcro® to the strips and think about how they easily stick together. Then separate them and insert another sentence strip without Velcro®, one with an unrelated sentence written on it. Since there is no sticking place, the unrelated sentence simply falls away. It does not cohere because there is no connection between it and either of the other sentences — it has no Velcro®. This is the difference between coherent and incoherent writing.

Like it or not, there are severe limits on your freedom as a writer. Writing without consideration of the reader leads to troublesome problems with coherence. Keeping the reader in mind, wanting the reader to *get it*, will help keep you focused and coherent. Deviating too far from the norms of correct English will result in incoherence and unintelligibility. The best way to reinforce coherence is to find examples in both fiction and nonfiction, and use those examples as models for practice. When you *borrow* these examples, to use Brancato's word from her book

*Borrowings*, you are rendering or innovating the text. This is a traditional way to experiment with sentence variety, structure, and coherence.

## Internal Coherence

INTERNAL COHERENCE refers to sentence-to-sentence cohesion, where one sentence coheres to another in a meaningful way. Sentence two connects to sentence one in some way. Sentence three to two and so on. There are different ways to create this Velcro® for sentences. I call them *chains*. Chains reinforce the idea that in well-constructed, logical writing, sentences link to each other like links in a chain.

## Vocabulary Chains

VOCABULARY CHAINS provide one way to maintain coherence. Using a word and then its synonym helps the reader follow the thought. For example:

> *Look at that old Ford. It looks like it belongs in a car cemetery.*

Often writers repeat a word to carry the sentences forward and keep them coherent.

> *Look at that old Ford — Ford windows, Ford upholstery, Ford everything. It looks like it belongs in a Ford cemetery.*

APPLICATION: Other vocabulary tricks used to maintain coherence, to forge those links of meaning, are antonyms, puns, plays on words, allusions, parenthetic utterances. See Paula Brock's book, *Nudges,* for ideas on how to employ and expand vocabulary.

# Sustained Thought Chains

SUSTAINED THOUGHT CHAINS furnish links from one sentence to another. In the opening chapter of *Girl in Hyacinth Blue,* Cornelius Engelbrecht and Richard discuss a rare painting that may be a Vermeer. Follow the thought chain:

> *"Look. Look at her eye. Like a pearl. Pearls were favorite items of Vermeer. The longing in her expression. And look at the Delft light spilling onto her forehead from the window." He took out his handkerchief and, careful not to touch the painting, wiped the frame, though I saw no dust at all. "See here," he said, "the grace of her hand, idle, palm up. How he consecrated a single moment in that hand. But more than that — "*
>
> *"Remarkable," I said. "Certainly done in the style of Vermeer. A beguiling imitation." (Vreeland, 4)*

Vreeland connects *eye* to *pearl*, *pearl* to *Vermeer*. *Eye* to her *expression*. *Light*, *hand*, all connected to the style of Vermeer, all a sustained thought.

APPLICATION: Use Vreeland as your model. Find a place in your writing to insert a thought chain.

#  *Grammatical Chains*

Just as chaining thoughts can link one sentence to another, so does chaining grammatical, syntactical, and lexical elements.

SPACE AND TIME WORDS:
> *We left our house in Houston in the morning. By evening, we were in Florida.*

By using the specific places—Houston and Florida—and the specific time—morning and evening, space and time are chained together making clear the leaving and the arriving.

DETERMINERS:
> *Some children like to play in the park. My child prefers his backyard.*

Determiners express quantity, number, possession, and definiteness (traditional grammars call these *adjectives*, e.g. *some, much, that, my*). They connect *some* children to the specificity of *my child*.

COMPARISONS/CONTRASTS:
> *Five children entered the writing contest. Austin Smith's entries were the best.*

Here the two statements fuse because of what is implied. Four children did not write the best entry; Austin did.

CONJUNCTIONS:
> *Many people complained about the loud music. And I did too.*

Perhaps the simplest chain is the coordinating conjunction. While perfectly permissible, this connector can be overdone. Other ways to bind thoughts need to be attempted.

CONNECTING ADVERBS:

> *I want to give you the background information. Briefly, I'll outline it here.*

Here the adverb *briefly* makes an observation about the condition of the background information.

> *Mary said she went to the opera. Confidentially, I think she went to a movie.*

Using the adverb *confidentially* suggests an interpretation. (Contemporary grammarians sometimes call these *disjuncts* because they express the conditions or make observations the reader should take into consideration.)

CAUSE AND EFFECT:

> *I went to the store because I needed milk for the baby.*
>
> *Because I needed milk for the baby, I went to the store.*

In each of the previous sentences the word *because* signals a connection between the two clauses. The subordinate clause *because I needed milk for the baby* provides the cause; the main clause supplies the effect. Sometimes writers think the cause must come first — not so.

APPLICATION: Noodle around with cause and effect sentences in normal and inverted order. Words and phrases that suggest cause are *since, as, whereas, inasmuch as, forasmuch as, due to the fact that, in view of the fact that, seeing that.*

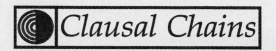

# Clausal Chains

*While Joe worked steadily in the garden, John went to the store to buy shovels. When he returned, Joe had finished. Then both of them began serious digging.*

Think of clauses as parts of sentences. They can either be independent (a mini-sentence) or dependent. When more than one clause is in a sentence, each must be joined to the other in some way. In the example above, the first sentence begins with a dependent clause, followed by a comma, and ends with an independent clause. The two clauses are knitted together by the association of *garden* with *shovels* and by the subordinating conjunction *while*, which suggests time. The pronoun *he* forms a link to the noun *John*, thereby connecting sentence two to sentence one. *Both* in the final sentence secures the two men with the action and ties the passage together satisfactorily.

APPLICATION: Examine your sentences. Be sure your independent clauses express your main ideas, while your dependent clauses express subordinate ideas.

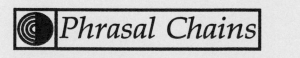

# Phrasal Chains

*The boys ran out of the building, across the street,*

*and into the shop on the corner. After buying their*
*materials, they headed away from school toward the*
*park.*

Stringing prepositional phrases to connect thoughts
and to sequence within sentences and from sentence to sentence works because prepositions, by definition, show relationship. Other phrases, such as adjectival, noun, or verb,
often bridge sentences to sentences in the same way that
words do; that is, by association or repetition.

APPLICATION: Check your phrases.  Do they connect?
Do they show relationships? Do they bridge?

# Parallel Chains

PARALLEL CHAINS link meaning through parallelisms.
Considered one of the most ancient and powerful ways to
organize sentences, parallelism gives corresponding sentences corresponding expression. In that way the brain connects the sentences and moves fluidly onward. My favorite
example of this comes from an eighteenth-century French
song that was used as background in the classic film *The*
*Heiress*, starring Olivia deHavilland.

*The pleasure of love lasts only a moment. The sor-*
*row of love lasts all life long.*

The noun *pleasure* is followed by the preposition phrase *of*
*love* followed by the verb *lasts*. The parallel sentence has the
noun *sorrow* followed by the same prepositional phrase and
the same verb. The twist comes with the final phrase which

makes a decidedly different statement.

APPLICATION: Choose a sentence from your writing. Follow it with another that uses the same structure. You may want to say the same thing or you may want to try a twist.

## *Pronominal Chains*

PRONOMINAL CHAINS are common yet effective ways to carry meaning forward without weak or boring repetition. Even little children have figured out this technique as in the following section of Asa's first grade story about being lost in Walmart:

> *I felt sad. I went to a manager, but she was busy. Another lady came and she said, 'Are you lost?' 'Yes.' She asked my name and my mom's name. She called Mom's name on the speakers and my mom came right away.*

Asa moves his story along in a coherent manner simply but using pronominal chains of *she*.

APPLICATION: Make certain you have used pronouns effectively and that the referent is always clear.

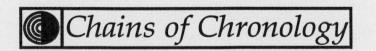
## *Chains of Chronology*

CHAINS OF CHRONOLOGY are the way we chronicle our

lives. You call a relative who asks how things are going. Most of the time that is an invitation to tell about your day. So what do you do? You begin when the excitement started or when the day began and sequence to the present. You use time signals to spur the telling forward. We find chains of chronology everywhere. Here is an example from *Galileo's Daughter: A Historical Memoir of Science, Faith, and Love* by Dava Sobel:

> *When Galileo was ten, he journeyed across Tuscany to join his parents and his infant sister, Virginia, in Florence. He attended grammar school near his new home until his thirteenth year, then moved into the Benedictine monastery at Vallombrosa to take instruction in Greek, Latin, and logic. Once there, he joined the order as a novice, hoping to become a monk himself, but his father wouldn't let him. Vincenzio withdrew Galileo and took him home, blaming an inflammation in the youth's eyes that required medical attention.*

Notice the subtle way Sobel sequences. Not using, *first, second, next, finally,* but with more sophisticated transitions and references to time such as: *When Galileo was ten, until his thirteenth year, then moved, Once there.* This level of sophistication is worth working toward through modeling and much writing.

APPLICATION: Check your writing for mundane words such as *first, second, finally*. Replace them with sophisticated transitional clauses and phrases.

# ⊚ *Punctuation Chains*

PUNCTUATION CHAINS are the tools of the writer. David Crystal in *The Cambridge Encyclopedia of the English Language* says of punctuation,

> *Its primary purpose is to enable stretches of written language to be read coherently, by displaying their grammatical structure.* (278)

PERIODS indicate a sentence ending so that the meaning of one sentence does not run into the meaning of another in a confusing way.

COMMAS divide words, phrases, and clauses to enhance clarity and emphasize meaning.

INDENTIONS mark topical paragraphs that contain a topic and supporting elements. Functional paragraphs are used by function: for changing speakers in dialogue, transitions, or for rhetorical emphasis. Each directs the reader to the path of meaning set out in the text.

APPLICATION: Reread your work focusing on its punctuation. Ask yourself, "Does every mark make my meaning clear?"

# ⊚ *Metaphoric Chains*

METAPHORIC CHAINS, sometimes called extended

metaphors, are not tricks of writing, but as John Frederick Nims sees it, "they are names for natural operations of the mind" (24). I like to say everything is a metaphor but the thing itself. Even language is a metaphor, with these squiggles representing something more. The word metaphor comes from the Greek and means *transfer,* so when we use metaphors we quite literally transfer one thing to something else. For example, this from an eighth grade student:

> *Missing school is a stub of the toe. First it hurts,*
> *then it throbs, and finally it's sore. Last time it hap-*
> *pened to me, my toe became so swollen I couldn't fit*
> *it into my shoe.*

The metaphoric chain begins with a simple comparision—missing school is like stubbing your toe. Then the chain begins to pin together a sequence of comparisons all related to the original metaphor: It hurts to be absent, the implication being that you miss out on whatever happened that day both in and out of class. The throbbing represents the pangs of guilt or worry associated with missed school, missed information, missed friends. The soreness suggests that there is an aftereffect. The next sentence in the chain acts as a summation. The student metaphorically states that returning takes some time to fit back in.

When I asked the young man why he chose this original metaphor to talk about so ordinary an experience, he said, "Just writing about missing school seemed boring. I wanted to jazz it up." Notice that as he "jazzed it up," he also added depth to his writing.

The bottom line: This is how you break down coherence to write it. This is how you learn the craft of working words, sentences, and paragraphs into a coherent composition. This is how you take the bits and pieces of the art form and carefully craft them into an integrated, harmonious whole.

APPLICATION: Find a metaphor in your writing. Extend it. See what happens to your meaning.

# Imagery Chains

IMAGERY CHAINS take an image, a mental picture, and multiply it in succeeding sentences. Most poems are imagery chains as they are often composed of a multiplicity of images. This wonderful poem "Saguaro" by Frank Asch piles image upon image as if growing the cactus. The placement of the words suggested by the physical shape of the poem visually reinforces the image of these ancient, tall cacti. (See the poem *Saguaro* on page 110.)

We expect imagery and image chains in poetry, so let us look in a place some might consider unlikely — a book of science. In Dennis Brindell Fradin's *The Planet Hunters*, I found this striking imagery chain about the Milky Way:

> *Often, at night, a white cloudy patch can be seen stretching across the sky. American Indians believed that it was the path dead souls followed to heaven. The ancient Greeks thought that it resembled spilled milk, which is why it became known as the Milky Way. When Galileo aimed his telescope at the Milky Way, he discovered that it is composed of*

**Saguaro**
Stand
still.
Grow
slow.
Lift
high
your arms to the sun.
Stand
still.
Grow
slow.
Lift
high
your
flowers to the sky.
Stand
still.
Grow
slow.
Hold
tight
your
water
inside.
Stand
still.
Grow
slow
and let your roots spread wide and let your roots spread wide.
—Frank Asch

stars *"so numerous as to be almost beyond belief."*
(20)

The *white cloudy patch* introduces the image and the
reader *sees* it *stretching across the sky.* The belief of the
American Indians and the Greeks extends that image — we
see souls trudging toward heaven; we see the spilt milk.
Finally, we see what Galileo saw — so many stars coalescing
to form that *white cloudy patch.* Again, in both the poem and
the prose, the imagery chain deepens understanding, mentally gives the reader more to gnaw on. That is what you
can do, with practice, in you writing.

In truth, you could create chains with most every
device known in *writingdom,* and the good writers do. By
practicing these chains you:

• Stay focused on the core of each sentence instead
of writing willy nilly whatever comes to mind;

• Take compositional risks by playing around with
language and the tools of language;

• Empower your writing;

• Engage in deeper thinking;

• Think about your writing in new ways;

• Produce coherent work;

• Become more skilled in the craft.

At first, be prepared for some bizarre metaphors,
mixed metaphors, dead metaphors, and just plain goofs.

APPLICATION: My advice is to always find an example
or two from literature. After analyzing the technique and
how it is executed in literature, write an original chain, one
you choose. Then do it again and again and again until you
can weave these chains into your writing with ease.

#  External Coherence

EXTERNAL COHERENCE functions the same way internal coherence does except, instead of connecting sentences, external coherence works with paragraphs. Each paragraph connects to the one before as well as the one after it. If you have been following formula writing, you may have forgotten this fact. You may think making three points or giving three events is all that is expected. Nothing could be further from the truth. If there are three points, or two points, or seventy-two points, each must be connected and all must relate to the purpose of the story, essay, poem—its proposition, its thesis, or its theme—whatever the genre. If there are three events or thirty-three, each must connect to each other to further the movement of the paper, to deepen it. These are not isolated points or events to be inserted to fill a page. If written with finesse, points or events become integral to the development of the thought in the work.

APPLICATION: Read each paragraph in your writing. As you move from one to the next, think about how you have connected it. If you don't find a connection, know your reader won't find one.

# Chapter 5
## On The Matter of Voice

*Regard your voice as
capital in the bank.*
—Lauritz Melchior

Voice in writing is as much its capital as Melchior reminds us it is in singing. It's the writer's stock, net worth, resource, principal asset, fortune, treasure—it's an advantage because it's a gain—it's the writer's wherewithal, the way to the means. But to truly have voice, you must have honesty. You have to speak from your bones and write from your heart. You can't write what you don't know, but if you try, you'll lose your voice. There's a lesson here. Don Murray says that:

> *Voice is often the force which drives a piece of writing forward, which illuminates the subject for the writer and for the reader.* (91)

Ralph Fletcher tells us:

> *Voice is far more than passion or charm; it is central to the learning process. Bill Martin has said that to really own information, to truly enter into the life of a story, poem, or novel, a writer must take the words of the text and transform those words in some way. When writers write with voice, they put the indelible stamp of their personalities on the information — they make it their own.* (79)

Little kids have voice. They "tell it like it is."

Janey, a five-year-old who quipped at breakfast,

> *When I'm not happy I'm like a doughnut without glaze*

has voice.

The second grader who described popping bubble gum in his mouth,

> *It feels like glue that you aksudentilly drank,*

has voice.

The voice of this sixth-grader is unmistakable:

*I swear, every day my sister takes soooo long getting dressed. She says it's because she has to keep up her image. What image?*

Sometimes kids retain their authentic voice as did this college freshman:

*"Twisted," "distorted," "grotesque'" — these are harsh words to say about someone you love, but they create an image of his body. You can see the pain in his eyes. He has trouble doing things that seem trivial to us. He seems like another man — feeble and old.*

*Although the memory is vague, I still remember when my grandfather was a strong hard-working farmer. He used to lift me up to the tractor seat and let me help plow. After all the chores were finished, it was time for fun. On this farm was the world's best fishin' hole. When we'd go there I got to ride in the back of the pickup. I didn't really like fishing, but I would do anything to be with him. Perhaps he felt the same because he didn't make me put those dirty worms on the hook or take those slimy fish off; he took care of that. Then something happened; he began to lose weight and his hands and feet became useless appendages. He would sit in his chair all day wringing his crippled hands refusing any help. He had too much pride.*

This introduces her research paper on arthritis and rheumatism. It's extensive writing, and it has voice. She concluded the paper by returning to the fishing hole. This time *she* puts the dirty worms on the hook and takes the slimy fish off.

Compare the writers above with the following examples of phony, faked, say-nothing, feel-nothing, word-wasting, pretend writing—what Ken Macrorie calls "Engfish" (1). These "Engfishy" writers tell it as they think people want it to be, or they want to impress people with their erudition. Soon the room and their writing becomes smelly with pretense.

Hold your nose before reading this description of class schedules written by a high school student. Lacking voice, it reads as if the student wrote with a thesaurus not a pen. Who is he trying to impress?

> For the most part, time plays a very, very portentous role in school. It tells us the regulations of each day. A class commences at a certain time and terminates at a predetermined place on the face of the clock. We embark on study each and every twenty-four hours accompanied by Father Time. Already we have begun to make out our orders for next year. These dicta are the foreordained times of the classes that we are obligated to enroll in order to move up the ladder of academic success.

Translation: We got our class schedules and have to figure them out before we graduate.

A Mom shared this next writing. As she talked, her eyes filled with tears. It seems her son loved to write, used to write long, imaginative stories that he excitedly shared with the family. Then he moved into fourth grade, a grade where the state-mandated writing test was administered.

There the teacher enforced formula. Mom said, "He has lost his voice not to mention his excitement. Look at this," she said sliding a paper across the desk. "He was supposed to write a composition for his teacher telling what he likes and doesn't like about birthday parties. He can do better than this."

> *Parties are fun becase there are food, games, and gift. Parties are for family and friends to be together to have fun and be happy. Parties can also bring lots of mess and you have to clean up. There can also be boring games and not get gifts. That can be a sad situation but the best part is to have fun.*

Translation: I wrote 'cause I had to write. The disengagement here is palpable. His paper lacks specificity at the onset: What kind of parties? He misspells *because* even though he can clearly spell *situation*. He leaves the *s* off *gift* and writes awkwardly and incoherently. Obviously, there is no connection to the prompt and little evidence that this young man once reveled in writing and delighted his family with his words. His mother was rightly concerned.

This sample from a middle school student wins the Engfish award for saying nothing:

> *English and science are both alike and different. In English I learn how to speak and write. In science we do things like read, write reports, and do experiments. There aren't many ways they are alike though. These are the ways English and science are alike and different.*

Translation: I counted the lines and restated the prompt, didn't I?

How's that for examples of the smelly stuff? If you are going to develop voice, you must first stamp out Engfish and get closer to good writing, writing that is vigorous, honest, alive, sensuous, unsentimental, unexpected, rhythmic, not pompous, fresh, metaphoric, evocative, economical, confident, and memorable. Macrorie would add "light" to this list. He tells us:

> <u>Hamlet</u>, *a story of decadence and tragedy, is at the same time one of the lightest plays ever written.* (23)

Honestly, wouldn't you rather read a text by Don Graves that begins:

> *Children want to write. They want to write the first day they attend school. This is no accident.* (3)

than one that starts:

> *If you are a student who desires assistance in order to write effectively and fluently, then this textbook is written for you.*

You hear Graves's voice in the first example; you smell Engfish in the second.

Peter Elbow says:

> *Writing with no voice is dead, mechanical, faceless. It lacks any sound. Writing with no voice <u>may</u> be saying something true, important, or new; it may be logically organized; it may even be a work of genius. But it is as though the words came through some kind of mixer rather than being uttered by a person.... Nobody is home here.*
>
> *Voice, in contrast, is what most people have in their speech but lack in their writing — namely, a*

*sound or texture – the sound of 'them.'... It's not*
*surprising that most people don't get voice into*
*their writing. Writing is so much slower and more*
*troublesome than speaking. So many more decisions*
*have to be made.* (287-89)

In order to get true in your writing, throw Engfish out.

# How to Get Rid of Engfish

To get true in writing does not mean baring your soul.
It does mean creating an authentic connection between
your writing and human experience. As Alfred Hitchcock
explains:

*... story can be an impossible one but it can never be*
*banal. It must be dramatic and human. What is*
*drama, after all, but life with the dull bits cut out.*
(71)

Aristotle phrases it paradoxically:

*The use of impossible probabilities is preferable to*
*that of unpersuasive possibilities.* (270)

Some suggestions:

• Practice the twin crafts of not wasting words but
elaborating fully.

• Lend a hand to a struggling writer who is trying to
uncover his or her authentic voice. When it glimmers into a
piece, encourage that voice. Helping others raises your
awareness.

• Read, read, read in order to discover how writers do

it, how they put the reader there so they'll believe.

• Read aloud and pause often to note word choice, coherence, figurative language. Note that causes have effects in writing both for the reader and for the writer.

• Play with tension. Play with oppositions that lead to surprise. Play with words.

• Find the satisfaction in building a piece of writing, not forcing some meaning into a form. Hold the jello not the mold.

• Ask or even demand something of the reader. Writing creates, but reading co-creates.

• Work for the sentence that sings. Work for the word that surprises. Work for the expression that delights. Work for the piece that has power.

• Write, write, write. Write what you know and move from that knowing into depth and breadth and cadence and precision and caring. Care deeply for your words on the page.

• Read Mem Fox's *Reading Magic*. Read it for all it says about reading; read it for its practical advice; read it for its suggested activities; but most of all, read it for its voice. Clearly, Fox has written from her heart and it shows in every line on every page.

• Use Eddie's question in *The Day Eddie Met the Author* by Louise Bordon to establish a friendly understanding of voice:

> *"How do you write books that have parts meant for me?"*
>
> *"Eddie, if you write about parts of yourself, I bet your reader will have some of those parts, too."*

To deepen that definition, connect it to what Pat Meehan says,

> *...a good writer must give part of herself away, must share with her readers if she is to be believed. She must have convictions, be strong, and show passion. She must define herself by speaking sincerely and truly about what she believes. She must shake out her deepest self.* (Fletcher and Portalupi, 54)

## Nonfiction

Authentic voice in extensive writing is no different than it is in reflexive writing. You simply have to own the information. Mostly what the inexperienced do when writing research is what Mary K. Healy, author of *Endangered Minds* and *Failure to Connect*, calls "dump-truck writing." They pick up a clump of information and drop those words into their papers. When you don't own or don't understand the information, you dump the clumps and push them together with wooden prose. The best antidote for that is reading great examples.

One of the best ways to understand voice is to study the difference between nonfiction writing with voice and nonfiction writing that is dry and boring. Take a nonfiction children's book about a subject and juxtapose it with the encyclopedic version. The following shows how one comparison stacks up.

SHARKS BY SEYMOUR SIMON. As you read the first four

paragraphs, note the lead, sentence length, incorporation of a statistic, transitions, comparison/contrast, alliteration, cause/effect, etymology of words, clauses, phrases, and elaboration.

*It never fails. You're at the ocean, swimming in the surf, and someone pretends to be a shark. They sing ominous music and then lunge at you.*

*People have always made up myths and legends about creatures they find mysterious and terrifying. Sensationalized books, television shows, and movies strengthen the myth that sharks are always on the lookout to attack people. The truth is that there are only about a dozen shark attacks in the United States each year (about 100 worldwide), and most victims live to tell their stories. In fact, you have a better chance of being hit by lightning than of being attacked by a shark. Sharks have killed fewer people in the United States in the past one hundred years than are killed in automobile accidents over a single holiday weekend. And no shark in the world counts people as part of its regular dinner menu.*

*When you know the truth about sharks, you'll begin to see them as the fascinating creatures they are, instead of the monsters of myth.*

*Sharks are fish, but they are very different from most fish. They belong to a class of fish known as "Chondrichthyes" (kon-DRIK-thees). The name comes from the Greek words "chondros," which means cartilage, and "ichthyus," which means fish. Like all fish, sharks have backbones, but unlike other*

> *fish, sharks have no other bones. Their skeletons are*
> *made of cartilage, a tough, white, flexible material*
> *just like the stuff at the end of your nose and in your*
> *ears.*

Follow that by looking at an excerpt on the same topic from an encyclopedia, in this case *The Concise Columbia Encyclopedia:*

> **shark** *predatory cartilaginous fish (order*
> *Selachii), found in all seas but most abundant in*
> *warm waters. About 250 species exist, ranging*
> *from the 2-ft (60-cm) pygmy shark to the 50-ft (15-*
> *m) whale shark. Sharks have pointed snouts and*
> *crescent-shaped mouths with several rows of sharp,*
> *triangular teeth. The most feared is the white shark,*
> *or maneater (Carcharodon carcharias), reaching 20*
> *ft (6 m) in length, which feeds on large fish and*
> *other animals and is known to attack swimmers and*
> *boats without provocation. Unlike other sharks, the*
> *whale shark and basking shark are harmless plank-*
> *ton feeders. Shark meat is nutritious, and shark oils*
> *are used in industry. Tanned sharkskin is a durable*
> *LEATHER. (768)*

While there is valuable information here, there is no voice, no attempt to draw the reader in or make the writing read as if written by another human being. Interestingly, most of this information appears in Simon's book but in a far more appealing way.

The point is that nonfiction can be as interesting as fiction.

# Other Books to Consult to Get Rid of Engfish

SCIENCE MODELS

Consider the fun of writing science research in the manner of Peter Sis's *Starry Messenger*. Compare it to the profound research done by Dava Sobel in *Galileo's Daughter*. The voices are different but equally interesting.

Patricia Lauber's *How Dinosaurs Came to Be* isn't some dusty tome, but a fascinating look and read, crammed with all kinds of information. Lauber says of her own writing,

> *Every book I write is about something that interests me.*

*Bugs* by Nancy Winslow Parker and Joan Richards Wright is a great model for the question/answer type of paragraph. It hooks the reader with a question and then reels them in with facts.

Be honest. How many of you know the word *xylem*? That is the word under X in David M. Schwartz's wonderful science alphabet book, *Q is for Quark!* Not only is this book rich in information, but what a wonderful idea for science class: Write an alphabet book about science using specific terms (works for other subjects, too).


ENGLISH/LANGUAGE ARTS MODELS

Regine Pernoud's *A Day With...*series contains many models within models: for example, *A Day with a Troubadour*. It begins with an introductory essay. Part One presents facts backed up with pictures, drawings, photographs, tidbits of information, and vocabulary laid out in an inviting way. Part Two tells the narrative but is punctuated with poetry. The Afterword is another essay. There is a Glossary, a Pronunciation Guide, a Further Reading List, and an Index. What a fabulous multigenre model this makes.

If *Shakespeare and Macbeth: The Story Behind the Play* by Stewart Ross were used as a model, it would shore up the old tried and true, dull and pedantic books on the Bard. Even the Foreword by Kenneth Branagh has voice.

> *The first I ever heard of William Shakespeare was*
> *when famous phrases or lines from his plays would*
> *appear on TV or in films, usually spoken by the*
> *great actor Laurence Olivier. Prince Hamlet's*
> *famous words, 'To be or not to be,' I first heard in a*
> *TV commercial for cigars!*

*The Divide* is the biography of Willa Cather by Michael Bedard, who also gave us *Emily*, the biography of Emily Dickinson. *The Divide* begins:

> *Willa stood at her window, looking one last time at*
> *the grass sloping down to the willowed stream, the*
> *road winding off into the wooded hills, the meadow*
> *marbled with sheep. Gone, forever gone.*

Use this model and apply its format to an author you are researching. Besides you get an extra dose of parallel structure and sentence length variety!

Speaking of biographies, here's a passage worth emulating,:

> *Late in the afternoon of July 9, 1948, Leroy 'Satchel'*

> *Paige began the long walk from the bullpen to the
> mound at Cleveland's Municipal Stadium. He did-
> n't hurry. He <u>never</u> hurried. As he said himself, he
> 'kept the juices flowing by jangling gently' as he
> moved. The crowd roared its appreciation. This was
> the fellow they'd come to see.*

Bill Littlefield tells the stories of ten remarkable athletes in
his book *Champions*, complete with Susan Butcher the
famous woman winner of the Iditarod Trail Sled Dog Race.

But voice doesn't get much better than in Robert
Burleigh's *Home Run*. It starts simply:

> *He is the Babe.*

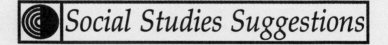

# Social Studies Suggestions

If the poignant photographs don't arouse interest in
David L. Parker's (with Lee Enger and Robert Conrow)
*Stolen Dreams: Portraits of Working Children*, the beginning
of Iqbal Masih's story will.

> *Each morning, six days a week, more than half a
> million children between the ages of four and four-
> teen rise before dawn and make their way along
> dark country roads leading to Pakistan's carpet fac-
> tories.*

There is also a story in the book which was written by
Belinda Quintanilla of Mission, Texas. It has voice.
Quintanilla owns the information; she's lived the experi-
ence.

Candlewick Press does a series of "Newspapers" that make great models for extensive writing with voice. In *Egyptian News*, headlines blare "Soaring Success," "Queen Rocks Nation," "Murder Foiled," and our favorite "Write to the Top," a story about being a government scribe. "It starts tough and gets worse!" begins this political page. Also on this page are ads. One placed by a "Qualified Scribe" offers a wide range of services; the other offers papyrus scrolls, inks, and even carrying cases "For Your Every Scribal Need." These books also show thematic connections.

David A. Adler paints powerful pictures with words in his Holocaust books. *Hilde and Eli* and *Child of the Warsaw Ghetto* illustrate how much research must happen to make writing come alive. Both are exemplars for showing the power of voice in historical fiction.

# How About Books on Mathematics?

But what of mathematics, you ask? Try *The Story of Money* by Betsy Maestro. What contemporary person could imagine life without money? This historical look at money provides an excellent example of taking something ordinary and making it interesting.

*Math Curse* by Jon Scieszka is the quintessential book to model if writing about math. Even the dedications are written in math lingo. But the opener is priceless, "On Monday in math class, Mrs. Fibonacci says, 'You know, you can think of almost everything as a math problem.' On Tuesday I start having problems." Perfect to model. Can't you hear the voice? I can. And how do you top a character named *Mrs. Fibonacci?*

## Art and Music Examples

*When Pigasso Met Mootisse* by Nina Laden is a funny look at two talented artists with lots of delightful word play. Best of all, Pigasso's dialogue doesn't sound like Mootisse and Mootisse's doesn't sound like Pigasso. It concludes with "The True Story of Picasso and Matisse," so the book blends fiction and nonfiction.

> *You walk into a gallery and find yourself face-to-face with Frankenstein's Monster!*

Not a bad beginning for a book entitled *The Painter's Eye: Learning to Look at Contemporary American Art,* right? Jan Greenberg and Sandra Jordan have executed the perfect book to point out voice when writing about art.

*Meet the Orchestra,* written by Ann Hayes, empowers the orchestra not only with music but also with great writing.

## Miscellaneous Fare

*Roller Coasters or I Had So Much Fun I Almost Puked* by Nick Cook offers deep research on roller coasters from the 1400 ice slides in Russia to La Vibora in Six Flags over

Texas. We hear the onomatopoeic "Clank! Clank! Clank!" and the "AAAEEEIIIYYY!" screams. Great book that kids love. And it's not booooorrrrrinnnng!

> *In a long room with seven tables and seven windows, a French monk sat hunched over a parchment page...*

so begins *Breaking into Print: Before and After the Invention of the Printing Press* by Stephen Krensky. What a wonderful model for a piece of research! What a wonderful model for a lead.

*Snapshot: America Discovers the Camera* by Kenneth P. Czech offers 19th and 20th century histories of the camera. Since clamps prevented people from moving while the chemicals, sunlight and lens worked the magic, the voice saying, "You can relax now," makes the reader do the same.

When you compare these and other well-written books to encyclopedia, typical historical texts, or textbooks, you recognize voice in the former and sterility in the latter. These are a small sampling of the wonderful children's books that offer just that.

Equally wonderful are the myriad young adult (YA) books written and available for every genre. Three examples:

*Great Puzzles of History: Intriguing Cases of the Past* by Fred Neff discusses ten historical controversies as varied as Robin Hood and Czar Alexander I of Russia. The prose is captivatingly straightforward, frittered with mystery. Chapter 3, entitled "The Missing English Princes," has an almost fairy tale quality. It begins:

> *A wooden chest containing the skeletons of two*

*children was discovered in the Tower of London by
a workman in July of 1674. Ever since that time
there has been speculation over whose remains were
found in the tower. Some people believe the skele-
tons were what is left of two missing English
princes known to history as Richard Duke of York
and the uncrowned King Edward V.*

Anne E. Neimark sets out the biography of Joy
Adamson, author of *Born Free*, in her book *Wild Heart*. Here
the genre, clearly biography, has some sections of dialogue
admittedly fictionalized, but most was found among
Adamson's writings. The book contains photographs
taken of baby lions, baby elephants, leopards, cheetahs,
and other animals Adamson rescued, sheltered, and stud-
ied in Kenya, Africa.

*Sinking to her knees beside Elsa as the three cubs
somersaulted over each other only a few feet away,
Joy wanted to thank her beloved lion for bringing
such treasures. "Your cubs," she whispered, her
eyes moist once again, "are wonderful! Adventures
await them, Elsa, in Meru Park--for they have what
you had but almost lost: They are 'free born.'*

*"And," Joy added as she gazed intently into
Elsa's eyes, "God willing, all of you will stay free."*

Another YA nonfiction book with punch is William
Loren Katz's *Black Indians: A Hidden Heritage*. This book—
which spawned documentaries, TV shows, magazine stories, songs, as well as other historical and cultural events—
opens with the question "Black Indians?" and concludes
with the saga of the great "Bull Dogger" Bill Pickett. The

book is filled with lively writing, fascinating facts, and great models to follow when writing creative nonfiction.

In his profile of Elizabeth Gilbert in *Poets & Writers*, Frank Bures credits Gilbert with breaking into the frontier of "creative nonfiction" or "the fourth genre" (32).

> *A friend of mine said, validly, "Just because it's nonfiction, and just because you're the narrator, doesn't mean you don't have an obligation to develop every character as though it were a novel. And just because you're the narrator doesn't mean you're not one of those characters." (34)*

David Snowdon, epidemiologist and author of *Aging with Grace*, the intriguing nun study that explores aging and Alzheimer's disease, offers a most creative prologue. He sets the stage for his factual study, but he also becomes one of the characters:

> *I recall a bright Saturday afternoon on a highway outside Redlands, California, my hometown. I'm five years old. My mother pilots our light green Ford Ranch wagon south toward San Diego. She is secretary to our parish priest, Father Henry Keane, and on this day she is chauffeuring five nuns who teach at Sacred Heart, the school where I will enroll the following year.*
>
> *It's 1957, and none of the sisters has a driver's license, much less a car. Two sisters sit up front with my mother and three sit in the backseat, lined up like fence posts in their full black-and-white wool serge habits. That leaves me, the little boy with the butch haircut, crammed into the rear luggage com-*

partment, the space usually reserved for our fox terrier, Spot. Broiling heat from the Santa Ana winds
cooks the car's interior, but the five overdressed sis-
ters remain stoic, their pale faces framed by the perfect ovals of their white wimples....

From my perch in the back, I peer out at the people in the passing cars. Most of them are tanned
and clothed in the diverse colors of southern
California. They turn with startled expressions to
stare into our old green boat, packed to the gunnels
with nuns. It is then that I realize that these brides
of Christ, who have taken vows of poverty, chastity,
and obedience, are as mysterious to most outsiders
as they are to me. It is as though they were inhabi-
tants of a different world. (1-2)

As Gilbert says, the techniques she uses to entice people into reading a story aren't so different from those used
to entice people into reading compelling nonfiction (34). In
other words, fiction or nonfiction, good writing is good
writing.

Julia Cameron, author of *The Right to Write*, reminds us:

My experience as a teacher tells me that it is never
too late for someone to find their writing voice.
Students of mine who began writing in their mid-
fifties have gone on to win playwrighting contests
and poetry festivals. A woman who took pen to
paper at seventy is publishing her first novel. All
too often what is missing in a voice is only confidence. (159)

In truth, all agree that voice is the single most necessary

quality that empowers writing with integrity. Without it, writing is nothing more than a recipe or an elongated verbal exercise.

I am fond of reminding others and myself that writing is hard work. Uncovering your voice is hard work. Description is hard work. Persuasion is hard work. Writing a story is hard work. Simply conveying the ephemeral in your head—thought—is hard work. So why do you do it? Because you are human and have a need to express what you think and feel. And, quite frankly, the closer you get those sometimes obstinate squiggles on the page to match your fleeting thoughts, the more satisfied you feel.

If you want to uncover your voice, you must read, read, read and write, write, write. Stephen King reminds us,

> *If you want to be a writer, you must do two things*
> *above all others: read a lot and write a lot. There's*
> *no way around these two things that I'm aware of,*
> *no short cut.* (145)

Writers must borrow and imitate; you must try and gag and try again. You must practice, practice, practice. The trick is to make the practice fun, challenging, engaging, and ultimately rewarding. Whoever heard of a football player who practiced yet never missed a touchdown? Whoever heard of a pianist who practiced yet never missed a note? Whoever heard of a lawyer who never lost a case, or a doctor who never lost a patient? What keeps the wheels going? Falling in love. Fall in love with the act of writing— those who do, make it.

##  *Application for Voice*

1. "BE YOURSELF." When you have voice, readers will recognize it. So voice must be organic to you. The reader wants you to sound genuine. William Zinsser emphasizes the need to be yourself,

> *Writing is, after all, a personal transaction between two people, even if it is conducted on paper, and the transaction will go well to the extent that it retains it humanity. Therefore I urge people to write in the first person — to use I and me and we and us.... Good writers are always visible just behind their words. If you aren't allowed to use I, at least think I while you write and then take the Is out. It will warm up your impersonal style.* (22 & 24)

2. BANISH:
- prepositions draped onto verbs, e.g. *head up*
- words that serve no purpose, *entire neighborhood*
- laborious phrases, *at the present time*
- ponderous euphemisms, *academic custodian*
- corporate language to hide mistakes, *downsizing*
- political language to hide mistakes, *counterforce deterrence*
- jargon, *instructional leaders*
- long words when short words will do, *individual*
- inflated phrases, *it should be pointed out that*
- swollen words and phrases, *sort of, kind of*
- diminishers, *little, rather, somewhat, slightly, maybe*

• intensifiers, *really, totally, very, deeply*

Replace these with what Ken Macrorie calls "meat and potatoes statements." Instead of: *I felt somewhat nauseated,* say it as it is, *I felt nauseated.* If you are nauseated, you are nauseated. The word *somewhat* just diminishes the statement. Instead of *She is very pretty,* say what you mean, *She is beautiful* or *exquisite, ethereal, gorgeous,* or even *pulchritudinous,* if that's the precise word and you own it, but trying to intensify *pretty* with the word *very* is flat out lazy and carries no voice.

3. COMB MAGAZINES, NEWSPAPERS, BOOKS, SIGNS, OR YOUR WRITING FOR EXAMPLES OF ENGFISH. This will heighten your awareness of how pompous, inauthentic writing smells. Then rewrite several in "meat and potatoes statements."

4. RELAX WHEN YOU WRITE. One way to relax in writing is by doing it often and in different ways. Write in journals, as responses to literature, literary letters to the authors you are reading, and you will find writing for any occasion less intimidating. Get into the habit of writing. Keep a writer's notebook for good stuff but collect lots of rubbish, too. Eventually this will lead to something good. Expose yourself to choices galore and multitudes of models. Learn to make savvy decisions. Writers who read as writers begin to write as readers.

5. DEVELOP A WRITER'S EAR. Make a phone out of a small piece of PVC pipe and two elbows for revisiting your writing. Whisper into the mouthpiece and hear your voice magnified in the earpiece. This helps tune up awks and frags, places where you preach, parts where you tell, tell, tell when you should show, show, show. Listen to hear if all

your characters sound the same. Listen for your voice.

6. TRY PREWRITING STRATEGIES: Remember a room in a school where you wrote your name as a child. Write your name holding the pencil in the "wrong" hand and imagine that room. Draw a floor plan. Put in the desks, chairs—everything you can recall. If you can't remember, pretend. How does it feel to be that pupil again? Write about it.

Another invitation comes from poet Wendy Barker in her book *Poems' Progress*. Barker suggests an excellent prompt, one that I have found results in authentic writing:

> *Think of an old toy you cherished, or one you always wanted but never received...and describe it.*
> *Write about what you now realize it represented to you as a child.*

I challenged myself to write to this prompt, called it "Toni" after my Toni doll. This piece also serves as an example of mixing genre—part memoir, part story, part informative essay—all working together to form a coherent composition. (See Appendix B.)

7. GIVE YOURSELF THE GIFT OF TIME, lots of time to think and write. Sit still a moment and listen to yourself speaking inside your head. When you hear a clear voice—be it happy, calm, excited, loving, irritated, angry, whatever—write.

8. WRITE TO AN AUDIENCE. John R. Trimble suggests two ways to develop voice:

> *Write with the assumption that your reader is a companionable friend with a warm sense of humor and an appreciation of simple straightforwardness. Write as if you were actually talking to that friend,*

*but talking with enough leisure to frame your*
*thoughts concisely and interestingly.* (77)

This might read: Write as if you are talking to your best friend in slow motion.

9. ESPOUSES DRAMA IN WRITING. Robert Frost says:

*Sentences are not different enough to hold the*
*attention unless they are dramatic. No ingenuity of*
*varying structure will do. All that can save them is*
*the speaking tone of voice somehow entangled in the*
*words and fastened to the page for the ear of the*
*imagination. That is all that can save poetry from*
*sing-song, all that can save prose from itself.*
(Introduction)

If you look for the tiny dramas in your life, you will find them — the box turtle that happened out from under the deck, the little Yorkie barking at the St. Bernard as the big dog backed away, the surprise in a crackerjack box, the unexpected phone call, the almost accident, the good feeling about something then the sudden shift in mood. Write what happens to you, write the facts, write what you remember, and eventually you will get inside the experience.

And kids can do that. First grader Patrick did. No phony baloney here:

*My hero is Dr. X. He is in Boston. He is a plas-*
*tic sergent. He put my lips together. And he is also*
*funny. He said when I come to Boston to bring him*
*a Big Red. Big Red is a soft drink.*

10. CONSIDER WRITING OUT OF "FABULOUS REALITIES." This phrase, coined by Ken Macrorie in the seventies, describes

an event when two ordinary things come together to explode in an extraordinary way. Look for these little surprises curled up in the bigger picture called life:

• Two obese men hang a billboard that reads: "Take the Fat Off!" A skinny foreman stands below and directs.

• The billboard advertises a hot dog stand with "Make it a Three-Dog Night."

• A business card reads, "Don Lighter, electrician."

• You hear an unexpected whizzing sound and realizing it's the crossfire of two gangs on opposite sides of the highway.

• Along a highway, a bearded man drags a huge wooden cross mounted on wheels.

Little kids notice things like

• Nana is wearing dinosaurs [earrings].

• This shell looks like a giraffe.

• The dog wasent normul. He was skaird of a frog!

• My enerjetic mother just served us nine pickles!

A keen writer's eye in life yields surprise when writing and adds voice.

# Chapter 6
## A Way to Keep Track

The one whose chariot is
driven by Reason
    And holds the reins of his
Mind,
    Reaches the end of the
journey.

—The Upanishads

# Deep Pockets

So you're deep into a manuscript, challenging yourself to go for depth by trying some of the suggestions in this book. Bravo! But how to keep track? Checklists can sometimes be helpful if used correctly, otherwise they bring about little change in a piece of writing. I've always been amused to read checklists for kids that list "spelling" or "punctuation." If students knew how to spell a word, it's unlikely they would intentionally misspell it; if students knew where to put that comma, it's unlikely they would omit it. It's just as unlikely, then, that they would spot the error. "Looks right to me," they say and check it off the list.

But "deep pockets" puts a different twist on checklists. They offer something different, a way to help you track your strategies and the ways you have deepened your writing. Best if all, they are easy.

APPLICATION: Get a library pocket, the 3.5" X 5" size—the brightly colored ones are best. Colors such as hot pink, lime green, luscious purple, teal, lemon yellow, citrus orange, neon blue keep your writing spirits up. Get a couple of colorful sentence strips—the 22.5" X 3" size works well. I've seen these in teacher supply stores, stationery stores, even grocery chains, and the big discount marts. If you cannot locate colored pockets and strips, no problem. Just use colorful markers to write on the manila ones or make the pockets by cutting legal-size envelopes in half.

Shave off the bottom of the pocket so that the sentence strip will go all the way through. On the front of the pocket, write *strategies & ways to deepen writing*. On one strip, list the strategies; on another strip, list the ways to deepen writing.

As your manuscript or manuscripts progress (you may want a separate deep pocket for each m.s.), check off the strategies and the ways you have worked to deepen your writing. This hands-on system is fun and satisfying. You'll also notice if you have a tendency to use one technique over and over again while ignoring others. That single observation  may help the effectiveness of your writing. If you see too much sameness, challenge yourself to try some other strategies, some other ways to deepen your writing. By manuscript's end, you should have tried various techniques. Thus, you have your own guide into writing with depth.

# Chapter 7
## Structure Underlying the Modes of Writing

Following a recipe never works. Words become brittle, won't pour into the mold we try so hard to fit them into. That's why writing from an outline usually produces something flat and formulaic.

—Georgia Heard,
*Writing Toward Home*

There is a big difference between structure and formula. Structure is the inherent, intrinsic backbone of writing, its foundation. It literally supports creativity because writers depend on it. Each mode in writing embraces its own basic structure, contains its own nerve center out of which radiates style and voice and purpose and meaning.

Formula, on the other hand, is prescriptive, allowing for little or no variation, therefore little or no creativity. The five paragraph paper is formulaic. Once a student told me she was required to write a five paragraph paper. "What if you only need four paragraphs?" I asked.

"I'll split one in two."

"And what if you need six?"

"Then I'll combine two paragraphs," she said with a toss of her head.

What is that all about? Certainly not about writing in real ways, and it certainly isn't about promoting good writing. Following a prescription is not learning the craft. Remembering the English teacher who proclaimed the dictum, "Every paragraph must have seven sentences," will shackle your mind. It's pure hogwash. Developing a sense when to fully develop an idea and when to let go comes closer to true writing. Because, in truth, there are few rules; there is only what works. As W. Somerset Maugham, once quipped,

> *There are three rules to writing the novel.*
> *Unfortunately, no one knows what they are.*
> (Brodie, 15)

Who wants to read a story or an essay that has every paragraph the exact same length?

So any discussion of structure brings us to *genre,* a French word that simply means category of literary composition.

The genres encountered most are:

| Fiction | Drama | Poetry | Nonfiction | Essay |
|---|---|---|---|---|
| Short story | Scripts | Narrative | Letter | Persuasive |
| | Plays | Lyric | Autobiography | Narrative |
| Novella | | Free verse | Biography | Definition |
| Novel | | | Memoir | Problem/Solution |
| Sudden fiction | | | | Classification |
| | | | | Compare/Contrast |
| Fables | | | | Informative |
| | | | | How-to |
| Myths | | | | |
| Tales | | | | Descriptive |
| Legends | | | | Documented |

As writers, you simply need to learn the basic structure of each genre. Then try your hand at variations.

# Thumbnail Structures

FICTION. At the most fundamental level, fiction is prose writing that has a beginning, middle, and end. These parts may be rearranged in any order. For example, flashbacks start *in medias res* or even at the end and double back.

Imaginary characters people the pages. Fiction has a setting, a plot or action that carries the story along, a problem and a solution.

DRAMA. Drama, a literary form designed for theater, written in script format, is usually meant to be performed by actors. Dramas range from classic Chronicle Plays to French *Comedia dell'Arte*, from Folk to Heroic Dramas, from Miracle and Morality Plays to Comedy and Tragedy.

POETRY.

> *Poetry might be defined as a kind of language that says more and says it more intensely than does ordinary language* (Perrine, 3).

This category of writing makes deliberate use of rhythm, rhyme, and figurative language to express deeper feelings than those usually conveyed in speech. It is most often written in stanzas with shorter lines than those of prose. Lyric poetry is more like song, is personal and individualistic, and is concerned with feeling. Free verse follows an open form allowing the poet to experiment with arrangement and form. Narrative poetry tells a story.

NONFICTION. Nonfiction, especially autobiography, biography, memoir, diary, journal writing, follows the structure of fiction, but, of course, deals not with imaginary but with real, actual events and the milieu of a person's life.

LETTERS. Letters have an internal structure of date, salutation, body, closing, signature. The formality differs with the nature of the letter, e.g. business versus friendly.

ESSAY. Essay holds to an introduction with a good lead, a body of supporting evidence, and a conclusion. (See Appendix C for Characteristics of Essays.)

Remember each genre builds upon its own structure. It's what the writer does within the structure that is important. There is a big difference between the love letters of drooling middle school students and the love letters between Pierre Ablelard and Heloise. There is a decided difference between a skit written for a high school fund raiser and Shakespeare's plays.

Most recently, writers are taking great liberties with genre, mixing them into what Tom Romano calls multi-genre.

> *Each genre offers me ways of seeing and understanding that others do not. I perceive the world through multiple genres. They shape my seeing. They define who I am* (109).

Antonia Susan Byatt's *Possession: A Romance,* qualifies as a multi-genre model. Within is a pastiche of letters, poems, stories, fairy tales, scholarly accounts, travelogues, touches of biography and mystery. This novel is deep and demanding with its rich, rich, rich allusions, symbolism, symmetries, and vocabulary.

A recent trend in young adult literature is what I call the poetic novel. The structure is that of a novel, but the text is written as poetry. *Love that Dog* by Sharon Creech, *Out of the Dust* by Karen Hesse, and *Bronx Masquerade* by Nikki Grimes are examples.

The more experience writers have with writing for different reasons, for different audiences, using different genres, the more proficient they become, the more they uncover their voices, the more satisfying writing becomes, and the deeper and less superficial is the writing. You will eventually find your genre. In the meantime TRY EVERY-THING!

> *I always know the ending;*
> *that's where I start.*
> —Toni Morrison

Adler, David A. *Hilde and Eli*. NY: Holiday House, 1994.

_____. *Child of the Warsaw Ghetto*. NY: Holiday House, 1995.

Adoff, A. (ed.) *I Am the Darker Brother*. NY: Simon & Schuster, 1997.

Ammon, Richard. *An Amish Wedding*. NY: Atheneum Books, 1998.

Arnold, Janis. *Daughters of Memory*. Chapel Hill, NC: Algonquin Books, 1991.

Asch, Frank. *Cactus Poems*. NY: Harcourt Brace & Company, 1998.

Barker, Wendy. *Poems' Progress*. Spring, TX: Absey & Co., 2002.

Barrett, Judi. *Cloudy with a Chance of Meatballs*. NY: Macmillan, 1978.

Baylor, Byrd. *I'm in Charge of Celebrations*. NY: Charles Scribner's Sons, 1986.

Bedard, Michael. *The Divide*. NY: Doubleday, 1997.

_____. *Emily*. NY: Doubleday, 1992.

Bordon, Louise. *The Day Eddie Met the Author*. NY: Margaret K. McElderry Books, 2001.

Boyle, T.C. *The Tortilla Curtain.* NY: Penguin, 1995.

Brancato, Claudia. *Borrowings.* Spring, TX: Absey & Co., 2002.

Brock, Paula. *Nudges.* Spring, TX: Absey & Co., 2002.

Brodie, Deborah. *Writing Changes Everything.* NY: St. Martin's Press, 1997.

Bruun, Erik. *Texas.* NY: Black Dog & Leventhal, 2001.

Bryan, Ashley. *Sing to the Sun.* NY: HarperCollins, 1992.

Bures, Frank. "In Search of the *Last American Man:* A Profile of Elizabeth Gilbert." *Poets & Writers,* (May/June, 2002): 32-39.

Byatt, A. S. (Antonia Susan) *Possession: A Romance.* NY: Random House (Modern Library Edition), 2000.

Cameron, Julia. *The Right to Write.* NY: Jeremy P. Tarcher/Putnam, 1998.

Carlson, L.M (ed.) *Cool Salsa.* NY: Holt, 1994.

Carroll, Joyce Armstrong & Edward E. Wilson. *Acts of Teaching: How to Teach Writing.* Englewood, CO: Teacher Ideas Press, 1993.

_____(eds.) *Poetry After Lunch.* Spring, TX: Absey & Co., 1997.

Catalanotto, Peter. *Emily's Art*. NY: Atheneum Books, 2001.

Charbula, Barbara.   *Before the Test*. Spring, TX: Absey & Co., 2002.

Cook, Nick. *Roller Coasters*. Minneapolis, MN: Carolrhoda Books, 1998.

Crane, Stephen. *The Red Badge of Courage*. NY: W.W. Norton & Co., 1962.

Creech, Sharon. *A Fine, Fine School*. NY: Joanna Cotler Books, 2001.

_____. *Love that Dog*. NY: Joanna Cotler Books, 2001.

Crystal, David. *The Cambridge Encyclopedia of The English Language*. NY: University of Cambridge, 1996.

Czech, Kenneth P. *Snapshot*. Minneapolis, MN: Lerner Publications Company, 1996.

Di Camillo, Kate. *Because of Winn-Dixie*. Cambridge, MA: Candlewick Press, 2000.

Elbow, Peter. *Writing with Power*. NY: Oxford University Press, 1981.

Espy, Willard R. *An Almanac of Words at Play*. NY: Clarkson N. Potter, Inc., 1975.

Estes, Clarissa Pinkola. *Women Who Run With the Wolves:*

*Myths and Stories of the Wild Woman Archetype.* NY: Ballantine Books, 1992.

Faukner, William. *Absalom, Absalom!* NY: Random House, 1951.

Fitch, Janet. *White Oleander.* NY: Little Brown and Company, 1999.

Fletcher, Ralph & Joann Portalupi. *Craft Lessons: Teaching Writing K-8.* ME: Stenhouse, 1998.

Fletcher, Ralph. *What a Writer Needs.* NH: Heinemann, 1993.

Fox, Mem. *Reading Magic.* NY: Harcourt, 2001.

Fradin, Dennis Brindell. *The Planet Hunters.* NY: Margaret K. McElderry, 1997.

Fritz, Jean. *Leonardo's Horse.* NY: G. P. Putnam's Sons, 2001.

Galarza, Ernesto. "Barrio Boy" in *Prentice Hall Literature.* NJ: Prentice Hall, 2000 (611-614).

Golden, Leon (translator). *Aristotle's Poetics.* NJ: Prentice-Hall, 1968.

Graves, Donald H. *Writing.* NH: Heinemann, 1983.

Greenberg, Jan and Sandra Jordan. *The Painter's Eye.* NY: Delacorte Press, 1991.

Grimes, Nikki. *Bronx Masquerade*. NY: Dial Books, 2002.

Hamilton, Jane. *A Map of the World*. NY: Doubleday, 1994.

Hayes, Ann. *Meet the Orchestra*. NY: Gulliver Books, 1991.

Heard, Georgia. *Writing Toward Home*. NH: Heinemann, 1995.

Hesse, Karen. *Out of the Dust*. NY: Scholastic, 1997.

Hobbs, Will. "Bringing Your Words to Life." *R & E Journal*. (Spring, 1996): 19-21.

_____. *Changes in Latitudes*. NY: Atheneum, 1988.

Hoose, Phillip. *We Were There, Too!* NY: Farrar Straus Giroux, 2001.

Hughes, Patrick. *More on Oxymoron*. NY: Penguin, 1983.

Janeczko, Paul B. (compiler). *Seeing the Blue Between*. Cambridge, MA: Candlewick, 2002.

Jiménez, Franciso. *Breaking Through*. Boston, MA: Houghton Mifflin Co., 2001.

Katz, William Loren. *Black Indians*. NY: Aladdin, 1997.

King, Stephen. *On Writing*. NY: Pocket Books, 2000.

Kingsolver, Barbara. *Prodigal Summer*. NY: HarperCollins,

2000.

Konigsburg, E. L. *The View from Saturday*. NY: Atheneum Books, 1996.

Krensky, Stephen. *Breaking into Print*. NY: Little, Brown and Company, 1996.

Kuralt, Charles. "Independence Hall" in *Prentice Hall Literature*. NJ: Prentice Hall, 2000 (604-606).

Laden, Nina. *When Pigasso Met Mootisse*. San Francisco, CA: Chronicle Books, 1998.

Lamott, Anne. *Bird by Bird*. NY: Pantheon Books, 1994.

Lane, Barry. *After the End*. NH: Heinemann, 1993.

Langer, Susanne K. *Philosophy in a New Key* (3rd ed). Cambridge, MA: Harvard U. Press, 1974.

Lauber, Patricia. *How Dinosaurs Came to Be*. NY: Simon & Schuster, 1996.

Levey, Judith S. (ed.) *The Concise Columbia Encyclopedia*. NY: Columbia U. Press, 1983.

Littlefield, Bill. *Champions*. NY: Little, Brown and Company, 1993.

Maestro, Betsy. *The Story of Money*. NY: Clarion Books, 1993.

Macrorie, Ken. *Telling Writing*. NY: Hayden Book Co., 1970.

MacDonald, Ann-Marie. *Fall on Your Knees*. NY: Simon & Schuster, 1996.

Martin, Bill Jr. and John Archambault. *Chicka Chicka Boom Boom*. NY: Simon and Schuster, 1989.

Mayer, Marianna. *Baba Yaga and Vasilisa the Brave*. NY: Morrow Junior Books, 1994.

Mora, Pat. *Confetti*. NY: Lee & Low, 1996.

Morrison, Toni. *The Bluest Eye*. NY: Plume, 1993.

Murray, Donald M. "Write Before Writing," in Carroll, Joyce Armstrong and Edward E. Wilson. *Acts of Teaching*. Englewood, CO: Teacher Idea Press, 1993.

Naylor, Phyllis Reynolds. *How I Came to Be a Writer*. New York: Aladdin, 2001.

Neff, Frank. *Great Puzzles of History*. Minneapolis, MN: Runestone Press, 1997.

Neimark, Anne E. *Wild Heart*. NY: Harcourt Brace & Co., 1999.

Nims, John Frederick. *Western Wind*. NY: Random House, 1974.

Nye, N. S. *Come with Me: Poems for a Journey.* NY: Greenwillow, 2000.

Oates, Joyce Carol. *We Were the Mulvaneys.* NY: Plume, 1997.

Orie, S. D. *Did You Hear Wind Sing Your Name?* NY: Walker, 1995.

Parker, David L. with Lee Engfer and Robert Conrow. *Stolen Dreams.* Minneapolis, MN: Lerner Publications, 1998.

Parker, Nancy Winslow and Joan Richards Wright. *Bugs.* NY: Mulberry Books, 1987.

Pernoud, Regine. *A Day with a Troubadour.* Minneapolis, MN: Runestone Press, 1997.

Perrine, Laurence. *Sound and Sense* (4th ed.). NY: Harcourt Brace Jovanovich, 1973.

Purves, Alan C. *How Porcupines Make Love.* MA: Xerox College Publishing, 1972.

Romano, Tom. *Writing with Passion.* NH: Heinemann, 1995.

Ross, Stewart. *Shakespeare and Macbeth.* NY: Viking, 1994.

Rossi, Joyce. *The Gullywasher.* Flagstaff, AZ: Northland Publishing, 1996.

Rowling, J. K. *Harry Potter and the Sorcerer's Stone.* NY: Arthur A. Levine, 1998.

Ryan, Pam Muñoz. *Esperanza Rising.* NY: Scholastic, 2000.

Schwartz, David M. *Q is for Quark.* Berkeley, CA: Tricycle, 2001.

Salinger, J.D. *The Catcher in the Rye.* NY: Little Brown and Company, 1945.

Scieszka, Jon. *Math Curse.* NY: Viking, 1995.

Shakespeare, William. *Othello.* New Haven, CT: Yale University Press, 1966.

_____. *Romeo and Juliet.* New Haven, CT: Yale University Press, 1966.

_____. *The Two Gentlemen of Verona.* New Haven, CT: Yale University Press, 1966.

Sierra, Judy. *The Oryx Multicultural Folktale Series: Cinderella.* Phoenix, AZ: The Oryx Press, 1992.

Simon, Seymour. *Sharks.* NY: HarperCollins, 1995.

Sis, Peter. *Starry Messenger.* NY: Farrar Straus Giroux, 1997.

Smith, Frank. *Writing and the Writer.* NY: Holt, Rinehart & Winston, 1982.

Snowdon, David. *Aging with Grace*. NY: Bantam, 2001.

Sobel, Dava. *Galileo's Daughter*. NY: Penguin, 2000.

Spinelli, Jerry. *Stargirl*. NY: Knopf, 2000.

Stanley, Diane and Peter Vennema. *Charles Dickens*. NY: Morrow, 1993.

Steedman, Scott. *Egyptian News*. Cambridge, MA: Candlewick, 1997.

Stevens, Janet and Susan Stevens Crummel. *Cook-A-Doodle-Doo!* NY: Harcourt Brace & Company, 1999.

Strong, Michael. *The Habit of Thought*. NC: New View, 1997.

Strunk, William Jr. and E. B. White. *The Elements of Style*. NY: Macmillan, 1972.

Suhor, Charles. "Linda's Rewrite," *Learning*. August/September, 1975, 20-25.

Tan, Amy. *The Bonesetter's Daughter*. NY: G. P. Putnam's Sons, 2001.

Tiedt, Iris McClellan. *Tiger Lilies, Toadstools, and Thunderbolts*. Newark, DE: IRA, 2002.

Trimble, John R. *Writing with Style*. NJ: Prentice-Hall, Inc., 1975.

Truffaut, Francois. *Hitchcock*. NY: Simon & Schuster, 1967.

Vreeland, Susan. *Girl in Hyacinth Blue*. NY: Penguin, 1999.
White, E.B. *Charlotte's Web*. NY: HarperCollins, 1952.

Winokur, Jon (compiler). *Advice to Writers*. NY: Pantheon, 1999.

Winthrop, Elizabeth. *Vasilissa the Beautiful*. NY: Harper Collins, 1991.

Yolen, Jane. *The Musicians of Bremen*. NY: Simon & Schuster, 1996.

Zinsser, William. *On Writing Well*. NY: Harper & Row, 1988.

PERMISSIONS

Asch, Frank. "Saguaro," from *Cactus Poems*. San Diego, CA: Harcourt Brace & Company, 1998. Reprinted with permission.

# 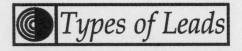 Types of Leads

### THE SUMMARY LEAD

Summarize or capsulize the topic in a few sentences and give the reader a picture of the scope of the writing.

### THE DESCRIPTIVE LEAD

Show the reader the locale of the piece, when the article is taking place, what the area looks like. Paint a picture in the reader's mind.

### THE MOSAIC LEAD

Overwhelm the reader with sentences, descriptions, images, impressions, fragments. Think of this complicated lead as a large mosaic on a wall. (Usually not undertaken by neophyte writers.)

### THE NARRATIVE LEAD

Tell a story within a story. Hook the reader with action, description, and color. Think of it as a short version of the longer story.

### THE ANECDOTAL LEAD

Show character, show personality, offer the reader a brief glimpse of the personality at work. Think of it as similar to the narrative lead but more as if you are talking directly to the reader.

THE PROBLEM (OR PARADOXICAL) LEAD

Show the problem in a situation. Pique the reader's curiosity about the problem.

THE FIRST PERSON (I) LEAD

Use your voice as writer/participant. Think of it as "this is what I say, did, mean."

THE SECOND PERSON (YOU) LEAD

Write as if you were having a casual face-to-face conversation with a friend. Think of it as "this is what will happen to you, this is what you will see and do, or this is how to do it."

THE INTERIOR MONOLOGUE LEAD

Only use if you know your subject inside and out. Present the thought processes, daydreams, ambitions, plans of the subject.

THE FLAT STATEMENT LEAD

Begin with a simple declarative statement. (Although this seems easy, the writing is better served with a more artistic lead.)

THE PARODY LEAD

Put a twist on song lyrics, a saying, or motto in order to establish a new perspective on the subject.

THE SIMILE OR METAPHOR LEAD

Ingeniously establish a comparison or relationship

between your topic/subject and something universally known.

### The "Flash" Lead

Disguise the true character, time, or location from the reader in order to maintain interest. (This is difficult since you do not want the reader to feel "taken.")

### The What–Where–When (newspaper) Lead

Use only for "news"-type writing or writing that you want to appear as news. Give the 5 W's and H in short sentences to quickly convey the facts of the piece.

### The Name-Prominent Lead

Give the name of the person or persons involved in the writing early in the lead. (This is especially good for famous or infamous persons.)

### The Diary–Timeline Lead

Use when showing change or progress over a length of time; use in the form of a diary entry.

### The Quotation Lead

Use an apt quotation to begin your piece.

### The Question Lead

Use an unusual, quirky, or thought-provoking question to kick off your piece. (Use sparingly. These leads usually sound phony.)

### THE DUAL NARRATIVE LEAD

This is a helpful lead when you have two trains of thought at work, e.g. balancing daily activities of one person against the daily activities of another.

### THE UNORTHODOX LEAD

When you are writing about someone or something that lends itself to something other than the typical conventional leads, e.g. something about film or a film star might begin with the word FADE IN and the lead might be written as a script.

### THE CLASSIFIED AD LEAD

Use a form of some newspaper column such as "Help Wanted" or "Houses for Sale." (This novelty beginning has almost become cliché, so beware.)

### THE FUTURE TENSE–FICTIONAL LEAD

When writing about something in the throes of change, consider an opening that is a "what if" speculative situation.

### THE SHOTGUN LEAD

Begin with multiple examples or multiple anecdotes which illuminate key facets of the piece.

### THE FLASHBACK LEAD

Begin in the past as a way to help explain a current situation.

### THE HISTORICAL PERSPECTIVE LEAD

Set up this lead as a way to connect the present with the past. Unlike the flashback, it begins in the present and connects it to the past.

### THE PSYCHOLOGICAL LEAD

Add a subtle load of psychological "baggage" to the more ordinary summary or description.

# 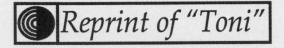 Reprint of "Toni"

> *"The desire for dolls is a manifestation of the human desire for beauty, which D. H. Lawrence once said we need more than bread. And the desire for beauty is akin to the desire for art, and for the sacred."*
>
> Wendy Barker,
> *Poems' Progress*

Secret ciphers. Sometimes they surface when I read. They seem to curl in, among, and between plaintext letters making the solid recognizable words different, bigger, somehow more, taking me beyond the squiggles on the page, turning the words into symbols of moments that spiral inside each other like those Russian nesting dolls.

This doesn't always happen, of course. Most of the time I read the words, comprehend them, and read on. Only when the secret ciphers appear for me to decipher, does the magic happen. It's always a surprise.

\* \* \*

I leaned into my task, eagerly. Here was a book of poems and essays so inviting I didn't mind the chore of proofing. After all this was the work of poet, Wendy Barker; her title, *Poems' Progress* promised delicious things.

Turning the pages from poems to essays, I marked a typo here and there. Perhaps I even made a suggestion. Then, like an unsuspecting innocent, I came upon "For Want of Dolls." In this poem and again in the essay following it, the secret ciphers lurked. They pitched me like Alice into a place where time reeled backward, a film unwinding itself. I half expected to meet the Mad Hatter. Holding on to Barker's manuscript as if my life depended upon it, as if I sat in the first seat of the most exciting roller coaster, I plummeted down the slide of memories into long ago.

It was a silly doll, really. A marketing tool for Ideal toys. A Toni Doll with magic "nylon" hair, a complete Toni play wave set which included 12 plastic curlers, 72 end tissues, creme shampoo, and a bottle of Toni play wave solution. Sillier still, I was in eighth grade, well past the age of playing with dolls, never mind curling a doll's hair. What obsessed me was my own hair. After all I was an adolescent when she arrived.

The launching moment was inauspicious enough: Mom was about to give me a home permanent. No longer, she explained into my thick mop of hair as she stood behind and above me, would I have to sit in Mrs. Kay's Beauty Shop "to look beautiful" under a machine that my memory tells me most closely resembled a huge metal octopus with tentacles of cords each ending with a metal clamp. "This is the newest thing--a permanent at home--and it will be easy," she said while I imagined most anything being easier than the torture of sitting for over an hour unable to move or read or do much of anything with pieces of my hair locked into each clamp.

Still Mom persisted. "This is a Toni home permanent. We'll get your hair all washed and clean and then just follow the directions."

Again the image of the alien cocoon filtered into my mind, heavy and even dangerous. Mom stopped sending me to Mrs. Kay's when she read about a woman getting electrocuted while sitting under one of those instruments of torment. Given the times, I imagined them in Nazi concentration camps, lined up against a cement wall with a prisoner under each. Here I was in the safety of my own home. How bad could this be?

While engaged in my reverie about my reverie, Mom began parting my hair into three sections: two sections bisecting my hair in front, and one long section which hung down my back. The pungent smell of lotion tickled my nose, but I was twelve and wanted to be beautiful. Playing with cotton and waving lotion, Mom managed to roll parts of my hair in the tiniest tissues, insert the hair into a tiny pink plastic curler with tinier teeth, swing its clasp up and over until it snapped into place. Since my hair was thick as wool, this procedure went on for what seemed like forever.

The next shock came with the wait. Mom's "easy" did not translate into "short." THREE HOURS! Three hours of expectation, worrying all the while if I'd come out beautiful or if I'd look like Bozo the Clown, a box of Brillo pads, or some cross between both!

Finally Brrrrinnng! the alarm clock Mom had set rang, and she began another procedure, this time putting water on the curlers. "Not finished?" I cried.

"No, we need to get every curl blotted and then a bit

damp, not wet."

That complete, Mom, as best I could tell, reversed the curler process and down came dampish, kinky, frizzy hair. I looked at myself in the mirror. I was fried, frizzled into a ball of fuzz! Bangs ran across my forehead like crimped wires. I looked frazzled and felt addled. I wanted to die. How could I ever leave the house again? I had become corrugated!

But those secret ciphers wouldn't stop. Nor did the Toni experience. Unbeknownst to me, a card had been enclosed in the permanent wave box for a Toni doll drawing, a marketing ploy no doubt. Mom fell for it, filled it out, sent it in. "For you," she said. Me, who didn't much play with dolls as a kid, too busy with hop scotch and ball blocks and Tarzan and the monkey bars. Too busy climbing trees, reading, writing stories, playing school. Me, who eschewed the twin dolls under the Christmas tree for the pile of games. Me?

I won.

In a neat gray and white striped box with pink everywhere, my Toni doll arrived. I tried to be excited for Mom's sake, but my own frizz was barely wearing off--the memory too keen--the luster of novelty home perms gone. Then I pulled off the lid of the box. Eyes closed, pouty red mouth, chestnut hair, she stretched one arm toward me--the winner. Instantly I fell in love with her. I loved her red leather shoes with the pewter metal snap in front and her gauzy red and white socks. I loved her white blouse trimmed in lace with dainty red rickrack at the neck and her blue cotton jumper trimmed in a yellow, red, and blue triangular pattern that connoted a bit of country. I loved her sweet face and that nylon hair, but most of all I loved her when she opened her bright blue eyes.

* * *

"Toni" is my acceptance of Barker's assignment. In her essay, she admits so strong a connection to the dolls in her poem that she began devising writing assignments based on an old cherished toy, one received or desired, one that now opens realizations of what that toy once represented.

What I know now that I didn't know then, couldn't have known then, rises up in me every time I see my Toni doll, even after all these years. When I first looked at her then, apparently the hormones of my adolescence screamed out. I saw her as a doll but loved her like a baby. She was not a toy, never a toy for me, but an awakening to the fact that all dolls represent babies, children. My future with children was thereafter marked because, as Barker says, "toys are metaphoric."

What I know now is that my desire for beauty through that annoying home permanent, as Lawrence tells it, indeed went deeper than the need for bread, and resulted in something more intense, richer and finer, something more profound than art, something buried at a depth almost--but not quite--indecipherable, but certainly something sacred.

–Joyce Armstrong Carroll

# Characteristics of Essays

| TYPE | PURPOSE | MAJOR CHARACTERISTIC |
|---|---|---|
| PERSUASIVE | • to persuade | • uses facts and opinions<br>• uses emotional arguments |
| HOW-TO | • to give steps or procedures | • linear steps from beginning to end<br>• sequence is important |
| NARRATIVE | • to tell a story | • personal in nature<br>• has a beginning, middle, and end<br>• uses flashbacks |
| DEFINITION | • to define an issue or problem | • has a clear bias<br>• has facts to support definition<br>• offers no solution |
| PROBLEM/ SOLUTION | • to consider a problem and offer a solution | • clearly states the problem<br>• considers causes of the problems<br>• offers at least one solution to the problem |

| COMPARISON/ CONTRAST | • to compare similarities and consider differences | • follows a pattern of comparison, such as 1.) first describing similarities in terms of elements of A compared to elements of B and then describing differences in terms of elments in B contrasted to elements in A. OR 2.) first describing all similarities in terms of A and B, then describing all differences in terms of A and B. OR 3.) taking a topical approach, describing similarities and differences of A and B in relation to each topic. |
|---|---|---|
| INFORMATIVE | • to inform | • clearly gives information |
| DESCRIPTIVE | • to describe an person, place, thing, or idea | • uses space, time, or or sequences |
| DOCUMENTED | • to accomplish any purpose | • uses quotations, facts, statistics from documented sources to support ideas. |